MIMESIS
INTERNATIONAL

T0027109

GEOGRAPHIES OF PSYCHOANALYSIS
n. 2

Directed by Lorena Preta

DISLOCATED SUBJECT

Edited by
Lorena Preta

MIMESIS
INTERNATIONAL

© 2018 – MIMESIS INTERNATIONAL (MILAN - UDINE)
www.mimesisinternational.com
e-mail: info@mimesisinternational.com

Isbn: 9788869771071
Book series: *Geographies of Psychoanalysis*, n. 2

© MIM Edizioni Srl
P.I. C.F. 02419370305

TABLE OF CONTENTS

ACKNOWLEDGEMENTS   7

INTRODUCTION: DISLOCATIONS   9
Lorena Preta

NO MAPS FOR THESE TERRITORIES.
BEING CARTOGRAPHERS OF SEXUALITIES TODAY   17
Vittorio Lingiardi

INTIMACIES OF TRANS-EMBODIMENTS IN IRAN:
TOWARDS AN 'ETHICS OF AMBIGUITY'   27
Gohar Homayounpour

BODY'S POLYSEMY AND THE RECENT CHANGES
IN THE HISTORY OF SENSITIVITY
Masculine, feminine and bisexual in today's world   51
Marcelo Viñar

THE INTIMACIES OF TRANS-LIVES   61
Jeanne Wolff Bernstein

ZOMBIE HYPERCALYPS(IS)   73
Paolo Fabbri

INTO THE DARKNESS. A TRIP THROUGH VIRTUAL SPACES   79
Mariano Horenstein

"THE TIME IS OUT OF JOINT". NEW SUBJECTIVITIES   95
Lorena Preta

AUTHORS   101

ACKNOWLEDGEMENTS

This book springs from a collaboration between the Geographies of Psychoanalysis Research Group and the Freud Museum in Vienna.

Felix de Mendelssohn, psychoanalyst, group analyst, university professor, intellectual concerned with Anthropology and with cultural interconnections, and active Museum board member, had the idea of organizing together an international meeting at the Museum. Along with Gohar Homayounpour, Museum board member and Founder of the Tehran Freudian Group, we began to brainstorm the meeting through the exchange of a series of intense, often witty, on the part of Felix, letterwritings, as was his style. Nearing the date of the meeting, however, Felix fell suddenly and gravely ill. Shortly thereafter, in the arc of a few short weeks, he passed away.

It is difficult to express in just a few words how painful this dramatic event was for all of us, however, I would like to bear witness as to how the gravity of his absence was mitigated by the group with a spirit of collaboration between all the participants and the organizers who set to work as if under his sort of protective wing.

I am deeply grateful to those who presented at the meeting, bringing with them the rich and courageous contributions which you will find in this book.

I would like to thank the Freud Museum director, Monika Pessler, who was an attentive and generous promoter of the meeting; Daniela Finzi, who patiently followed all the organizational phases from the beginning; Esther Hutfless and Victor Blüml, who coordinated and introduced the reports of the day, and finally, Natascha Halbauer, for the coordination of the secretariat.

INTRODUCTION
DISLOCATIONS

LORENA PRETA

"A stamping ground for wild asses"

There are historical times where cultural paradigms and different behavior models seem to contrast, as if each represented a true alternative to the one preceding it, so marking a definitive and radical change. These different facets offered by reality may be considered as violent contrapositions of the preceding establishment, or on the other hand, it may be denied that they be representative of anything new and be considered only as contingent versions of the same phenomena; or still, they may be given a futuristic version, as of something still needing to evolve and that will be manifest in its true meaning, only in time.

In this way, there are alternative interpretations of events, which are seen as either sudden and catastrophic caesuras or on the contrary, as lines of continuity which blend the boundaries of civilizations, the ones into the others, across the constant redefinition of mobile frontiers.[1]

Certainly what can be gathered is that every new establishment which makes its way into history is the product of tireless, social and individual destruction and transformation of the work preceding it.

This is a complex and dramatic process which constantly moves the boundaries of time and space between events and confuses the meanings we give them. As a result, we are occasionally driven to either including events in what is already existing or to refusing them; or otherwise still, to recovering them from the past and propelling them, without any processing, into the future, until we assemble completely new ones, eradicated and disconnected from any history or context.

Decompositions which appear to be arbitrary and disturbing or which provoke an inert indifference. One can occasionally feel pulled away from one's own place of origin, dislocated elsewhere, without being able to recompose a sense of personal existence and of the history to which one belongs.

---

1   Silvia Ronchey, *Chalk Lines*, in *Geographies of Psychoanalysis: Encounters between cultures in Teheran*, ed. by Lorena Preta (Milan-Udine: Mimesis International, 2015).

Yet within such a critical picture, it is worth remembering that it is by giving value to eccentricity, mobility, liminal distribution, that we are able to make our mental boundaries permeable and to confront alterity, in all its forms.

Is not the transference mechanism, to mention one of the pillars of psychoanalysis, a dislocation which allows us to place life experiences and temporal diachronies on an object, which cannot overlie past experiences and yet it is an access to sentiments and emotions which would otherwise remain unexpressed? A complex phenomenon which encloses much more valence in the psychoanalytic picture and has specific functions but which is the basis of every cognitive and affective experience.

We therefore need to consider more than one aspect of the dislocation phenomenon, a metaphor allowing us to draw the process, even physically. The main actor of this scene is without doubt the body. It is in relation to the body and its technological manipulations that we measure the most perturbing changes which today's society offers us, in all countries of the world, albeit in different forms.

For many years already, our vision of the body and the procedures we have so far used to understand and describe it, have been upturned. This causes unsettlement and disorientation and often, as a reaction, we feel reassured by taking for granted and as already acquired, behaviors which on the contrary are entirely new and still need to be understood and analyzed, possibly with knowledge that guarantees us a sufficient complexity and practices that we know and belong to us. Psychoanalysis is one of these.

We could also say that the body is strongly on the scene because there is a tendency to place problems on it, which should rely on a psychic elaboration.

This denounces an insufficiency of the symbolic function which is without doubt a characteristic of contemporary society.

However, it is necessary to keep in mind that also thanks to psychoanalysis, precisely the progress of knowledge on the most primitive states of the mind and the precocious phases of development, together with the insight provided by the anthropological analysis of the various forms of bodily expression, intended as socially structured languages, has increasingly brought to consider the body as a bearer of a multiple and complex capacity of expression.

In this same direction go the neurobiological researches, when they do not strive to create mechanistic correspondences between the physical plane and the mental or psychic planes. They describe a plastic mind, in constant redefinition with respect to the phases of development and to the surrounding environment, which is able to organize highly diverse communicative modules.

Therefore, we are now more able to take on the body in its complexity and to make it a "speaking" subject.

Yet the reasoning expressed by Foucault[2] on the new alliance which took place at the end of the XVIII century, between *words and things*, as a result of the possibility to observe the body scientifically, somehow contributed to overcoming the subject-object dichotomy. It helped to observe and speak of body and illness in a different way and appears now to be measured with fragmented and composite identities, whereby life experiences of the body prevail, reified or propelled in an increasingly distant and disembodied virtuality.

Once more the body runs the risk of being imagined more than seen, inserted in a "visionary space" where all attributions are possible.[3] The desire or drive inhabiting it, find immediate realization on the plane of reality and drive up newly repainting, at least apparently so, biological pictures and historic characteristics which are already given, following individual or social drives.

Yet it is this same awareness which should induce us not to ignore the meanings deriving from the various psychological and social issues which the bodies propose. Precisely because we know that every gesture in reality introduces an expressive and communicative dimension, which is the product of dense interweaving between the individual and culture and which cannot be reduced to the need of satisfying a desire or exercising a personal right.

Psychic organizations of desire, transformed into socially applicable rights, are cultural expressions which may be either encouraged or repressed, from time to time, but it is precisely their historically determined character which should encourage to steer away from solutions that are obvious or dominated by prejudice.

Indeed we often see that even the most reckless issues, which come out as perturbing novelties on the scene, once they have completed their positive function of deconstructing the most rooted and undisputed customs, they then impose themselves as new unquestionable models.

On the other hand, the alterity inhabiting us in a substantial way, represents the *aporìa* around which, despite everything, we define and build our self and possibly, for this very reason, it should in some measure, remain unresolved. It would instead appear necessary to maintain the *tension* which characterizes, each time, the process of acknowledgment or expulsion of parts of the self which are negated or unexplored.

This same process would appear to count for the meeting with the foreignness of the external world.

---

2   Michel Foucault, *The Birth of the Clinic: An Archaeology of Medical Perception* (London, 1973).

3   Please see Lorena Preta, 'Editoriale', 'Corpi e controcorpi', Psiche, 1 (2003), Il Saggiatore, Milan.

This may be applied, firstly, to all those changes which relate to sexuality. Can we find today a place for sexuality or as Vittorio Lingiardi says, "we do not have maps for these territories"?

"Nowadays sexuality seems to be dislocated, more than marginalized". Indeed, it is sexuality itself which is not only dislocated but also "dislocating", always. This feature of sexuality, allows it to constantly unbalance the obviousness of visions which are shared socially.

Discussion on the origins of sexual behaviours, for a start homosexuality and the fact that we question its etiology, turns it into a pathology itself. Furthermore, it is considered either in its genetic component, or on the contrary, as totally relational and dependent on family dynamics.

The boundaries are instead more undefined and fluid. The author invites us to keep a flexibility between the various positions, a tension allowing for "standing in the space".

The analysis by Gohar Homayounpour, inserts itself into this debate contributing a height of observation and claiming to subvert the discussion on difference. The issue of transgender people, described in the situation of a country like Iran, where homosexuality is punished with prison, if not with death penalties, becomes the paradigm of how it is possible to solve in a definite and denying way, the perturbation which accompanies the issue of transexuality.

Considered as a degeneration, the obstacle is overcome, inducing and encouraging transgender people to undergo surgery, in order to obtain the sex they desire and so reach a definition of gender which is final and stable. Through a documented series of statistics and interviews, Homayounpour brings us to consider how the indetermination of the sexual condition, may not be eluded with a drastic physical solution, which will apparently remove ambiguity but it must be borne and revived, allowing it to be enigmatic "towards an ethics of ambiguity".

Many interferences appear between the desiring subjectivity, which suffers because it is perceived as dislocated, projected towards an alterity which is lived internally, as a presence which is more real than what the genetic body and cultural construction define, and the demand for conformity to traditional social conduct.

Yet, on the basis of this experience, we may ask how we can contribute to avoiding the risk of finding ourselves in a closed world, which finds meaning only for the single individual, where our personal experience, our personal inclination will ultimately reinforce a situation of isolation and where a detachment will continue, between the social and the individual imaginary with which we should indeed come to terms by accepting a two-way co-construction, between the individual and society.

Often we seem to find ourselves confronted with the need to claim identity, which expresses the unsustainability of the co-presence of alterity, firstly within the subject itself and ultimately colluding, as in a paradox, with that same aforementioned intolerance of society, for ambiguity, multiplicity and difference.

However, for the constitution itself of desire, the size of prohibition seems unavoidable, as we are reminded by Marcelo Vinãr. Yet how can we keep alive the interaction between what is prohibited, even if pertaining to the individuality of the subject and the claim for personal freedom of choice?

Phantasies on sexuality, familiar relationships and all that today seems to be on the scene in such a new way, have always been the basis of our psychic life, but before they seemed to refer mostly to the private side and not the public one. The "radical changes are not necessarily parallel (or in linear causality) with the internal experience".

Therefore we are left with a gap, a discrepancy between the present culture, the ways in which it manifests itself and the deep reality of the psyche.

It is necessary at this point, not to chase the present, acting hastily but to use psychoanalytic experience for "reestablishing a healthier equilibrium between the transitive (or explosive) times and the reflexive ones of the psychic experience".

In any event, the body we are talking about, is a body, as we often said, which is increasingly fragmented. Even on a literally physical plane, we can dismantle it and substitute its parts with both human and animal or mechanical pieces. These are life experiences which no longer refer to mythology or to our phantasmatic world but to our daily experience.

At the basis of these practices, we find however, a mythology which glorifies "partiality" and makes it an apparently adequate solution to the demands of time, but which sacrifices the contrasting idea of an "entirety", where the deep need for integration is more acknowledged.

We live in the world of "pluriverse", we surely cannot cancel the awareness of multi-dimensionality, both psychic and cultural, both geographic and geopolitical, in which we are immersed, but we must not for this reason sacrifice a complete vision of the living and of its surrounding environment, which aspires to the complexity of a whole, composed of numerous heterogeneities, yet without renouncing its coherence.

This disintegrating fragmentation rather seems linked to a death drive. Just as in a nightmare or in the most extreme horror phantasies, we find ourselves dealing with removed organs, inserted in foreign bodies which must be "convinced" to accept the alien body part with massive therapies.

We use innovative fertilization techniques which allow a woman to incubate an embryo created elsewhere, in vitro, or in any case, a product of material assembled from bodies unknown to each other. Then when this is all measured with trade and with selling for necessity, with the power of wealth and with the desperation of poverty, how can we not think that we are dealing with a phase in the history of humanity, where we can no longer take anything for granted.

Exploitation walks besides generosity and love, hope and therapy with desperation, experience and personal motivation with the compulsion to conform.

Where does the subject place itself in this setting? What definition may we give it with respect to a presumed other than the self?

"Subjectivity is ultimately located so far outside of a self that the self can only survive as an object, an instrument and a mere function both in the eyes of the Other and subsequently of the subject himself" says Jeanne Wolff Bernstein. Tracing the path of the history of transplants and the more recent one of surrogate motherhood, not only do the most extreme phantasies find application, says Bernstein, but also some mechanisms such as the incorporation and introjection, are measured with the new experiences that technologies offer, fusing these psychic functions with the process of mourning.

A failed, unprocessed mourning, such as the one which is forced upon us by the speed of change and the disappearance of a sense of limit.

Indeed as we have observed, the psychic and social container, composed of the Oedipal triad and of the diverse sexuality connected to it, on which for centuries the scheme representing reality was based, at least in western society, has suffered a crisis. This has dismantled the sense of time which is no longer defined by generational conflict or sexual diversity.

At the moment, it is difficult to say whether there is a replacement of these psychic assumptions, through their transformation or if they remain functioning but disguised by altered forms.

We can link this phenomena to how death is viewed in today's society. It appears to be considered as an unacceptable condition to fight against even when faced with forms of life which are no longer definable as such; with bodies kept alive artificially which are far from recalling the individual's existence as it was before, if not for the possible physical resemblance of bodily features.

Phenomena which appear to be connected not only by the lack of limit, by omnipotence and obsessiveness but also by a sense of time which is similar to a phantasy of Eternity, which denies the desire itself of death as a finish line to reach at the end of a track.

According to Freud, the death drive is not contradicted by the instinct for life but rather "the organism wishes to die in its own way"[4] and it tries to accomplish this; complex and contorted ways which reach for the same objective, namely to get there.

We also know that immortality would not ensure happiness for man, it would instead deprive him of his emotional and affective characteristics, as the sense of life is defined from the horizon of death.

One has the prevailing impression that experiences are not directly experimented, affected by that alexithymia, a new pathology of the present time, which makes emotional participation impossible, or that they are only "hallucinated" and unable to meet with reality.

We are disconcerted by violent actions which besides having historic and so cultural and political motivation, bring us back to that irreducible area of the psyche, characterized by a destruction process with no return. Yet we must at least question the new forms it takes in the present to try to distinguish, differentiate and help us understand.

The past indeed appears to present itself in the form of an apparent revenant where we must recognize the changes it carries and so the anticipations of an uncertain but already active future.

The hybridization forms which we know in today's society have no preceding ones in the history of humanity so much so that they radically change our concept of what is human.

We witness a "hybrid cross between human and inhuman" as Paolo Fabbri reminds us, in such a way that we can observe the construction of a new myth which not only "does not meld nature and culture, the animate and the inanimate, but situates itself between life and death: the zombie."

"Icons of globalization", witnesses of suburban decadence, the zombies enact the decay of the bodies and the orgiastic drive, "the individual necrosis and collective narcosis".

These living dead spread in a viral way with their ability to bring back the dead on the scene of life. "Now the Undead add an inescapable 'historical' interrogative to the present of the living: how do we live with the experiences of the past? Without the pressure of planning for the future?"

---

4   S. Freud (1920), 'Al di là del principio di piacere', in *OSF*, vol. 9 (Turin: Bollati Boringhieri, 1997), pp. 64, 65.

The forms of virtual communication also provide evidence in a dramatic way of the body's dislocation. The various forms which it takes, from the web to Facebook, to Youtube, Instagram, Snapchat, represent a journey "into the darkness", suggests Mariano Horenstein.

The journey to Dante's inferno with the rounds which are increasingly nearer the substantial impossibility of describing the "virtualized body" of new technologies; as well as the one Borges describes in the auto-generating and hypertextual universes, which self-create the very space containing them in a game of endless recall, describes in an intense and suggestive way the novelty of this revolution of communication.

Psychoanalysis, as both a theory and a practice, appears to be anachronistic with respect to this and absolutely "against the tide", but only in this way "we can hear some things like the crackling noise of the needle on an old vinyl record", a remnant as anachronistic and mysterious as the words with which psychoanalysis is accustomed to work.

The consequence of all that we have attempted to describe seems to be that we have become inhabitants of a space "beyond time", whence we can neither reach the past, nor imagine a future.

A world made of an unburied humanity which survives as it waits for prolonged youth which however no longer returns; as it waits for work which cannot be obtained, for an uncertain sexuality which no longer defines anything or close to it, for redemption from historic injustices which created indefinability and rancor, and for an end which no longer belongs to the whole body as it has been intended so far.

A dislocated life, no longer centered but not marginalized either. No longer belonging only to the individual but also to the community from which mostly it appears to be disconnected.[5]

Perhaps we can do no more than try to find a processing area for this condition, where the turbulence owed to change can find a closed space to evolve without being obscured and overcome. If psychoanalysis is ready to measure itself with this, then it can still offer some possibility.

> If psychoanalytic intuition does not provide a stamping ground for wild asses, where is a zoo to be found to preserve the species? Conversely, if the environment is tolerant, what is to happen to the 'great hunters' who lie unrevealed or reburied"[6]

---

5   See Lorena Preta, 'Fuori dal tempo', in *Vivere/ Sopravvivere*, ed. by Alfredo Lombardozzi, Edizioni Alpes, forthcoming.

6   Wilfred R. Bion, *A Memoir of the Future, The Dream*, vol. 12 (Karnac Books, 1991), p. 15.

NO MAPS FOR THESE TERRITORIES. BEING CARTOGRAPHERS OF SEXUALITIES TODAY

Vittorio Lingiardi

> None of us want to be in calm waters all our lives.
>
> Jane Austen, *Persuasion*

"Has sexuality anything to do with psychoanalysis?" is the challenging title given by André Green (1995) to a paper in which he stated that "direct discussion of sexuality seems to have declined in ordinary clinical presentations, and sexuality also seems to have become marginalized" (p. 871). In my opinion, nowadays sexuality seems to be more dislocated than marginalized, both from a theoretical and a physical (bodies, environments, places ...) perspective. Do we still have a "located" and "only one" model of psychosexuality? Do we still have a specific place where sexuality can express itself? Do we have, I would say, a clear definition of what "sexuality" is? Or, with the complicity of the queer theory,[1] we can only talk about "sexualities" giving up unequivocal definitions? Are we able to develop a model of mind that can "account for the great variety that marks the relationship between gender, psychological equilibrium, and the indistinguishable work of cultural regulation?" (Corbett, 2008, p. 849; see also Corbett, 2009).

---

1   *Queer studies* are the studies of issues relating to sexual orientation and gender identity usually focusing on lesbian, gay, transgender, queer, questioning and intersex people and cultures. Questioning sexual labels, queer studies deal with multiple and creative forms of desire and its objects, where queer means not only "strange, oblique, eccentric" but also "doubtful unclear, deviant" and "faggot". As noted by the Italian philosopher Adriana Cavarero (1996, p. VIII), "due to our language is heterosexually-driven, queer language seems to be an insult. It is on this point that queer theory stresses its attention. It does not challenge the repulsive effect of the term "queer" — its definition of an abject and terrifying other — but it radicalizes its meaning in a positive one. The definition of queer as anomal, eccentric, marginal, terrifying turns into a political issue of identification that criticizes the universality (and naturalness) of the heterosexual paradigm. This operation is obviously made possible, rather encouraged by post-structuralist horizon that characterizes all the radical expressions of American thought".

Clinical practice and empirical research on the origins of sexual orientation, as well as gender and cultural studies have now shown that our sexualities and genders are developmental and relational constructions: simultaneously both biological and social, both inventive and defensive. They result from genetic and hormonal predispositions, family expectations and social pressures, conflicts and defences, fantasies, identifications and counteridentifications, projections and introjections. They arise from the incessant attempt to come to terms with one's own pleasures, anxieties, identities and compromising solutions. Rapid and unpredictable transformations are now changing our cultures and sexualities: lesbian, gay, bisexual, transgender, transsexual, and queer identities; new family forms resulting from new possibilities of conception and filiation; cyber- and chat- sexualities. Yes, chat-sexualities: a new dislocation of sexuality, made up of dissociation, displacement, diversion, leisure time, compulsivity, addiction, playfulness ... *action in virtuality*.

In order to put sexuality to the heart of the discussion, we need to recall some "fragments d'un discours" sexuel (Barthes, 1977) that has challenged psychoanalytic bedrocks over time — such as the role of culture over "natural facts" of sexuality and the relationship between gender expression and sexual orientation.

Culture and the "natural facts" of sexuality

"I write poetry because my genes and chromosomes fall in love with young men, not young women." With this carefree and cheerful verse, Allen Ginsberg (1994) screws up centuries of dispute about the role that nature and culture play in our lives. But, we know that poets follow idiosyncratic and arcane thinking. Sooner or later people ask: "Are homosexuals born that way or do they become homosexuals through outside influences?". This usually means: "Is homosexuality caused by primary relationships and family structures? Or is it just a matter of genes and hormones?". This question is inescapable but wrong because it is affected by two prejudices: first, we are all born as tabulae rasae, ready to be shaped by external forces. Second, we are born already programmed for specific tastes, desires and behaviors. But binary oppositions — such as nature vs. culture, inside vs. outside, black vs. white – are always wrong. Life is made up of shades, and hopefully not always fifty and gray. Moreover, this etiological conundrum becomes inevitably etiopathogenetic because it pushes us to see homosexuality and heterosexuality as the effect of something that went wrong in one case and something that went as it should in the other. In a clinical context, in fact, the heteronormative germ often lurks just in the attempt to "find a cause" to "explain" why a person is homosexual. People (and psychoanalysis) don't ask, "Why are you straight?" but many times homosexual people ask themselves, "How did I become gay? How did I become lesbian?". In addition to gender stress (Drescher, 1998) and minority stress (Meyer, 2007), we should take into account the *etio(patho) logical stress*.

Sexual orientation and gender construction

One more question. Does the orientation of our *sexuality* have to do with the construction and expression of our *gender*? The multiplicity of meanings contained in those two embodied concepts is a definite obstacle for a full understanding of the relationship that unites and separates them.

So, the first answer should be no – everybody knows that gender expression and sexual orientation are two independent dimensions. Rather, for a long time, psychoanalytic theorization about homosexuality has overlapped male homosexuality with "femininity" and female homosexuality with "masculinity". This overlapping, based on a binary and stereotyped idea of "masculine" and "feminine", has nevertheless delayed the theorization both of gender and sexual orientation. Homosexual men, for example, have been thought to be "failed women", a sort of "sub-gender", losing the inevitable weave of their sexualities, cultures, personal styles. Instead of using "homosexuality" as a way of de-binarizing gender categories, also revealing the inadequacy of the category of "heterosexuality", it has been used as a way for confirming gender binarism (Lingiardi, 2007). Rather than exploring the experience of homosexuals to broaden the categories of gender, psychoanalysts "have restricted the possibilities of gender to the conventional heterosexual masculine/feminine binary" (Corbett, 1993, p. 346).

The second answer should be yes, and in any case — homosexuals or heterosexuals. The relationship between gender and sexual orientation is a topic too often approached in a polarized way — we should be able to understand it with a more dialectical attitude. They cannot overlap completely or be separated categorically, and they cannot be read wearing only one type of glasses: biological, psychological or social. "The challenge is neither to essentialize gender nor to dematerialize it", as said by Muriel Dimen and Virginia Goldner (2012, p. 135; see also Dimen, Goldner, 2010).

Sexual orientation and gender expression are not connected in a forced and predictable way. Personal histories and cultural inscriptions influence the gender shadows by which the individual expresses her/his desires. We know that there is no gender that is "expressed" by actions, gestures, or speech. Rather, its performance is precisely that which retroactively produces the illusion that there was an inner gender core (Butler, 1990, 1999). So, when we are thinking about gender, we cannot make reference to a template. Gender is something we do rather than something we are. Even the idea of a "natural body" that is pre-existent to its discursive productions and cultural inscriptions is illusory. Gender can be culturally forced, but it is also individually shaped and personally interpreted — among the others, see gay bears or twinkies, metrosexual men, transexual people. Gender as a soft assembly. "Gender can be a rich playground or a desert, a stark cartoon or highly elaborated spaces in mind, body and life [...] Gender may be softly assembled, but it is also a work in progress" (Harris, 2005, pp. 151, 173).

As part of this work in progress, we should consider dislocation of our sexualities also from a strictly geographical perspective. What was the impact, on non-Western cultures, of sexuality and gender as they have developed in the Western cultures since the last century? Should we answer in terms of a destiny of colonization, assimilation, globalization or, at the moment, are we exploring a patchy territory where the binary code of a monotheistic self coexists with multiple and more fluid selves? Or, maybe, has the history of sexualities its origins in a history of dislocations of which the first, resounding, dislocation has been that from the male narrative of sexuality (including that of female sexuality) to a sexuality "in a woman's voice"?

The current landscape is constituted of acres of fundamentalism with many postmodern settlements. This image could also be described as an imagination-in-progress of the unconscious, seen not as a melting pot where distinctions dissolve but as a mosaic containing disparate aspects of a single self; not something layered like an onion or like an archeological site, but a kaleidoscope, a complex organization in which a series of elements with different shapes and densities re-shuffles itself into unique structures determined by the pathways of infinite relationships.

Increasing attention towards that which is relative, constructed, and multiple has changed the way we analysts see the structure of the psyche and its development. With the establishment of a "decentered" view of the self, mental functions are now seen as a configuration of changing states of consciousness that are discontinuous and non-linear, in dialectical relation with the necessary idea — the healthy illusion — of a unitary self.

My generation is still marked (scarred) by psychoanalytical certainties that are too often entangled in the conviction that psychoanalysis must promote particular values; but many of us, fortunately, have been trained with the wise idea that the best that an analyst can hope for is an "uneasy co-existence of a multiplicity of epistemologies" (Ogden interviewed by Mitchell, 1991, p. 369).

Trying to integrate fragments into the discourse

According to Christopher Bollas (1992), sexuality has so many different shapes that trying to hold them together in a comprehensive theory succeeds only at the cost of a grave distortion of the differences which exist between individuals. In her book *The Enigma of Desire*, Galit Atlas (2016) offers an original construction of sexuality as located in the tension between Enigmatic and Pragmatic dimensions, challenging the binaries of known and unknown, seen and unseen, internal and external, masculine and feminine, and oedipal and pre-oedipal experiences of the body. Moreover, we should realize that sexualities are nowadays more and more intertwined with cybersexualities and assisted reproduction technologies are changing our conception of filiation (Lingiardi, Carone, 2016; Lingiardi et al., 2016).

I am aware that when we talk about sexuality any unidirectional theory risks to be misleading and dangerous. Sexuality can be thought as a double helix developing over time along an "evolutionary trajectory", and at the same time nourishing itself of a dialectic between part objects and whole objects; pre-oedipal and oedipal elements; oral, anal, phallic and genital elements; self-regulation and mutual regulation; autoeroticism and object relations. So, my idea is that the subject is dislocated also because sexuality is dislocated, and dislocating.

As a sort of unconclusive conclusion, I will introduce some food for thought to reflect on sexuality today. I like the way Winnicott refers to "psyche" as the "imaginative elaboration of somatic parts, feelings, and functions" (1949, p. 243). We should think to first body experiences (feeding, evacuation, pain, pleasure, etc.) as "organizers" of the more complex and narratively structured subsequent experiences that flow into the "idiom" of our sexuality. Moreover, adult sexuality contains residues of early intersubjective exchanges between caregiver and infant. In this sense, mother-infant mutual regulation and recognition can be considered as a container for sexuality — and for the "too muchness" of excitement associated with it, as said by Benjamin and Atlas (2015), following

Laplanche's (1992, 1995) and Ruth Stein's idea (1998, 2008) of excess as enigmatic message. Inhibitions and facilitations promoted by our caregivers connect pleasure-seeking with myriad affective states, often with a sexual connotation, such as embarrassment, humiliation, shame, guilt, and so on.

From an attachment perspective, Fonagy (2008) suggests that caregivers tend to (defensively?) ignore or minimize the sexual feelings of the child. "The vast majority of mothers — he says (p. 22) — claim to often or mostly look away in response to the sexual excitement of their infants, whether girls or boys". In this way the infant's experience is not mirrored, recognized and given back to the infant as worthy of symbolization and thought. These feelings remain "dissociated" within the attachment bonds and, as a consequence, sexuality remains "dysregulated". Therefore we hope that our lovers see what has not been seen originally and mirror our desire in a way that... when our lovers touch us, they touch both our desire and our grief, awakening our pleasure and our pain at the same time.

The role of motivational systems is another important topic. Motivational systems, be they are five (Lichtenberg, 1989) or seven (Panksepp, Biven, 2012), are associated with specific neurophysiological patterns and are based on behavior observable in the neonatal period (the need to fulfill physiological requirements, the need for attachment and affiliation, the need for assertion and exploration, the need to react aversively through antagonism and/or withdrawal, and the need for sensual and sexual pleasure). The cooperative or alternative relationship (a sort of psycho-physiological dance) between these systems influences our search for a partner and our sexuality (think, for example, the conflict between the attachment–affiliation system and the sensual–sexual one). In the context of interpersonal relationships, the satisfaction and the balance of these systems promote experiences that give strength and cohesion to the Self through sexuality.

Sexuality also means privacy, secrecy, phantasy, and exploration — all elements that can allow unexpected expression of ourselves and experiences free from censorship or conditioning (see, for example, the many selves of a cybernaut of sexuality) (Lingiardi, 2008, 2011). In this regard, as analysts we should be able to assess when virtual reality is a space that "opens up new kinds of fantasy and relational possibilities or is the net a snare, [...] a retreat from both psychological and social relations to a dissociative place of suspended animation and compulsive usage?" (Hartman, 2011, p. 477).

Why sexuality has something to do with psychoanalysis...

In keeping with the previous "fragments", we can now answer to the first question: "Has sexuality anything to do with psychoanalysis?". Yes, it does as sex(uality) is a powerful organizer of the (psychic) experience. "The fact that sexuality entails an interpenetration of bodies and needs — Mitchell wrote (1988) — makes its endless variations ideally suited to represent longings, conflicts, and negotiations in the relations between self and others" (p. 103). At the same time, I feel that if we reduce all to the past and present relational configurations, we would lose "something" of the physical reality of sexuality. This is as if in this "physicality" there is always an element separated (splitted, dissociated or removed) from those inspiring configurations that now lives their own lives.

While we are exploring, we have also to tolerate that "sex trades on the thrill of discovering, over and over again, that we are unknown to ourselves" (Goldner, 2003, p. 123). Working psychoanalytically on sexuality looks like working psychoanalytically on dreams. Something remains unexplored, there is at least one spot in every sexuality "at which it is unplumbable — a navel, as it were, that is its point of contact with the unknown" (Freud, 1900, p. 111).

As clinicians, we have the possibility to help people not only to recognize and follow the directions of their own desires, but also to compose the absolutely personal sense of identity among gender, sexual orientation, and social culture. We have to work for the integration of the fluid and flexible components of identity with those ones needing stability and shared definitions. The challenge ahead is capturing the different states of mind without dropping that "-s". Considering potentially healthy and potentially pathological instability as well as rigidity. Assimilating variance without repudiating sameness. Admitting the tension between what we have and what we are missing. Grasping the singularity of each condition and, at the same time, recognising the contingencies that qualify that condition, making it plural.

Everything permanent, everything that belongs to the hardening of our habits, must be made fluid; everything volatile and uncertain must be anchored and solidified. Tension — the oscillation between relative and absolute — will guide us on the search for idiomatic pathways that can sustain our creations of gender and sexuality. It is in this capacity, both individual and social, to "standing in the spaces" (Bromberg, 1998) that we determine whether we are working on an idiomatic solution or an exile from ourselves.

References

Atlas, G., *The Enigma of Desire: Sex, Longing and Belonging in Psychoanalysis* (New York & London: Routledge, 2016).

Barthes, R. [1977], *A Lover's Discourse: Fragments*, transl. by Richard Howard (New York: Farrar, Straus and Giroux, 1978).

Benjamin, J., Atlas, G., 'The 'too muchness' of excitement: Sexuality in light of excess, attachment and affect regulation.', International Journal of Psychoanalysis, 96 (2015), 39–63.

Bollas, C., *Being a Character. Psychoanalysis and Self Experiences* (London: Routledge, 1992).

Bromberg, P.M., *Standing in the Spaces: Essays on Clinical Process, Trauma and Dissociation* (Hillsdale, NJ: The Analytic Press, 1998).

Butler, J., *Gender Trouble. Feminism and the Subversion of Identity* (New York-London: Routledge, 1990).

— —, 'Preface', in *Gender Trouble. Feminism and the Subversion of Identity* (New York-London: Routledge, 1999).

Cavarero, A. (1996), 'Preface to the Italian edition', in Butler, J., *Corpi che contano* [*Bodies that matter*], (Milan: Feltrinelli, 1993).

Corbett, K., 'The Mystery of Homosexuality', Psychoanalytic Psychology, 10, 3 (1993), 345–357.

— —, 'Gender Now', Psychoanalytic Dialogues, 18 (2008), 838–856.

— —, *Boyhoods. Rethinking Masculinities* (New Haven: Yale University Press, 2009).

Dimen, M., Goldner, V. (eds.), *Gender in Psychoanalytic Space: Between Clinic and Culture*, 2nd ed. (New York: Other Press, 2010).

— — (2012), 'Gender and Sexuality', in Gabbard, G.O., Litowitz, B.E., and Williams, P., *Textbook of Psychoanalysis*, 2nd ed. (Arlington, VA: American Psychiatric Publishing), pp. 133–154.

Drescher, J., *Psychoanalytic Therapy and the Gay Man* (Hillsdale, NJ: The Analytic Press, 1998).

Fonagy, P., 'A genuinely developmental theory of sexual enjoyment and its implications for psychoanalytic technique', Journal of the American Psychoanalytic Association, 56 (2008), 11–36.

Freud, S., 'The Interpretation of Dreams', in *Standard Edition*, vol. 4 & 5 (London: Hogarth Press, 1900).

Goldner, V., 'Ironic Gender/Authentic Sex', Studies in Gender and Sexuality, 4, 2 (2003), 113–139.

Ginsberg, A., *Cosmopolitan Greetings* (New York: Harper Collins, 1994).

Green, A., 'Has sexuality anything to do with psychoanalysis?', International Journal of Psychoanalysis, 76 (1995), 871–883.

Harris, A., *Gender as Soft Assembly* (Hillsdale, NJ: The Analytic Press, 2005).

Hartman, S., 'Reality 2.0: When loss is lost', Psychoanalytic Dialogues, 21, 4 (2011), 468–482.

Laplanche, J., *Le Primat de l'autre en psychanalyse* (Paris: Flammarion, 1992).

— —, 'Seduction, persecution, revelation', International Journal of Psychoanalysis, 76 (1995), 663–82.

Lichtenberg, J.D., *Psychoanalysis and Motivational Systems* (Hillsdale, NJ: The Analytic Press, 1989).

Lingiardi, V., 'Dreaming Gender: Restoration and Transformation', Studies in Gender and Sexuality, 8, 4 (2007), 313–331.

— —, 'Playing with unreality: Transference and Computer', International Journal of Psychoanalysis, 89, 1 (2008), 111–126.

— —, 'Realities in dialogue: Commentary on Paper by Stephen Hartman', Psychoanalytic Dialogues, 21, 4 (2011), 483–495.

— — (2015a), 'No maps for uncharted lands. What does gender expression have to do with sexual orientation?', in Lemma, A., Lynch, P. (eds.), *Sexualities: Contemporary Psychoanalytic Perspectives* (New York: Routledge), pp. 101–120.

— — (2015b), 'Born this way? La scienza dell'orientamento sessuale e le sue implicazioni' [Born this way? The science of sexual orientation and its implications], Preface to the Italian edition, in LeVay, S., *Gay, straight and the reason why. The science of sexual orientation* (Milan: Raffaello Cortina, 2011), pp. IX–XXV.

Lingiardi, V., Carone, N., 'Lesbian mothers, gay fathers: an unconceivable conception?', Giornale Italiano di Psicologia, 43 (2016), 57–79.

Lingiardi, V., Carone, N., Morelli, M., Baiocco, R., '"It's a bit too much fathering this seed": the meaning making of the sperm donor in Italian lesbian mother families', Reproductive BioMedicine Online, 33 (2016), 412–424.

Meyer, I.H., 'Prejudice and discrimination as social stressors', in I.H. Meyer, M.E. Northridge (eds.), *The Health of Sexual Minorities. Public Health Perspectives on Lesbian, Gay, Bisexual, Transgender Populations* (New York: Springer, 2007).

Mitchell, S.A., *Relational Concepts in Psychoanalysis* (Cambridge, MA: Harvard University Press, 1988).

— —, 'An interview with Thomas Ogden', Psychoanalytic Dialogues, 1, 3 (1991), 361–376.

Panksepp, J., Biven, L., *The Archaeology of Mind: Neuroevolutionary Origins of Human Emotion* (New York: W. W. Norton & Company, 2012).

Stein, R., 'The poignant, the excessive and the enigmatic in sexuality', International Journal of Psychoanalysis, 79 (1998), 259–68.

— —, 'The otherness of sexuality: Excess', Journal of the American Psychoanalytic Association, 56 (2010), 43–71.

Winnicott, D.W. (1949), 'Mind and its relation to the psyche-soma', Read at the medical section of the British Psychological Society, First published on British Journal of Medical Psychology, 27 (1954). Republished in *Through Pediatrics to Psychoanalysis* (London: Tavistock Publications, 1958).

INTIMACIES OF TRANS-EMBODIMENTS IN IRAN: TOWARDS AN 'ETHICS OF AMBIGUITY'

GOHAR HOMAYOUNPOUR

Abstract

The intimacies of trans-embodiments within contemporary psychoanalysis have suffered from a binary approach towards the transsexual trajectory.

On one hand, psychoanalysts basing their work on a reductionist reading of Freud have applied a heteronormative discourse, of pathologizing and moralizing attitudes. On the other hand, in more recent years psychoanalytic literature has taken a turn towards a 'transgenderity' filled with a politically correct and at times superficial humanitarian discourse of sameness.

It is the author's assertion that both of these approaches operate in the name of sameness and normalizing, a far cry from a subversive psychoanalytic discourse of difference.

This paper will use some clinical material around trans-embodiments in Iran, as well as other narratives such as interviews and two documentaries, in an attempt to move towards a subversive psychoanalytic discourse of unfamiliarity and ambiguity, from the standpoint of geographies of transgenderity.

Introduction: Transgenderity in Iran

While is important not to turn away from the significant work of activists and some psychoanalysts in recent years, we need to move towards a more refined and sophisticated understanding of trans-embodiments.

The particular situation of trans-embodiments within the specific geography of Iran will be used to demonstrate a point around this politics of difference. The specificity of the situation will highlight the more universal problem of contemporary psychoanalytic discourse regarding trans-embodiments.

In 1987, Maryam Khatoon Molkara was the first person to meet
Ayatollah Khomeini to obtain a letter which acted as a Fatwa enabling sex
reassignment surgeries if confirmed by a specialist doctor.

Ms Molkara, who had formerly been called Fereydoon, wrote a letter in
1975 to Ayatollah Khomeini who was then in exile in Najaf: he answered
as follows. "You must observe all the rites specific to women." Ms Molkara
was finally able to meet Ayatollah Khomeini in 1987, after her request was
studied by clerics and doctors. She obtained the Fatwa (a ruling on Islamic
law given by a recognized authority): "Gender reassignment, if prescribed
by a trusted doctor, is not against *Sharia* [the body of Islamic law]." (Trait,
2005).

Ever since this Fatwa, Iran's Islamic government recognizes people with
sexual-identity disorders and SRS is a choice approved by the government.
Transgender people are also offered new birth certificates. Some are now
even recommended by clerics for treatment, and the government helps
to fund a portion of the costs of the operations. Before the 1979 Islamic
Revolution, there had been no particular policy regarding transsexual and
transgender people. (McDowall, A. & Khan, S., 2004).

Khabar Online, a very popular Iranian news website, announced in a
report based on statistics compiled by the *Legal Medicine Organization*
that the number of requests for sex reassignment procedures is rising every
year in Iran (Khabar Online 2012).

Year	Frequency	Male to female		Female to male	
		No	Percent	No	Percent
2006	170	101	59/41	69	40/59
2007	297	201	67/67	96	32/32
2008	294	175	59/52	119	40/47
2009	286	133	46/50	153	53/49
2010	319	158	49/52	161	50/47
Total	1366	768	56/22	598	43/77

Figure 1: Quantitative analysis from data of individuals with Gender Identity Disorder
(ILMO, 2011)

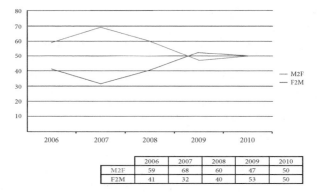

	2006	2007	2008	2009	2010
M2F	59	68	60	47	50
F2M	41	32	40	53	50

Figure 2: M-to-F, and F-to-M ratios between 2006 and 2010 (ILMO, 2011)

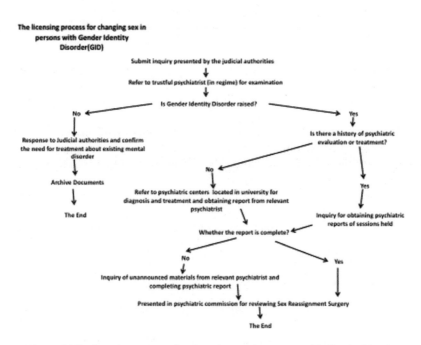

Figure 3: The licensing process for changing sex in persons with Gender Identity Disorder (GID) (ILMO, 2011)

According to the Legal Medicine Organization, 1366 gender reassignment procedures were conducted in Iran between 2006 and 2010: 56% of which were female-to-male and 44% male-to-female reassignments. Over 270 Iranians go through the sex reassignment procedure every year (Khabar Online, 2012).

Official statistics indicate that between 15,000 and 20,000 transsexual people currently live in Iran; however, unofficial estimates place the *Trans* population of Iran at 150,000 (Trait, 2007).

There are two official associations with permission from the Ministry of Interior to work to support people with gender dysphoria. The *Special Committee for Gender Dysphoria* of the Mashhad University of Medical Sciences has evaluated 38 cases in the last three months, among which there were 20 male-to-female cases and 18 female-to-male. The objective of this institution is to identify, organize, protect and treat people with gender dysphoria.

The founders of this association are a group of psychiatrists and psychologists in the Legal Medicine Organization, and a group of social activists. They seek to support *Trans* people socially, legally and financially in order to help them establish a stable and independent life after sex reassignment operations.

This provides a very interesting background to the analysis of trans-embodiments. In a conservative country where the state is run through religious laws, we have what, at least on the surface, seems to be a liberal law.

They are two points that can be highlighted here. Firstly, the rising numbers, as can be observed in Figures 1 and 2 above: in Iran we have the largest number of 'sex change' operations of any other country except Thailand. Secondly, according to the statistics there are more male-to-female sex change operations than female-to-male. The causes of this phenomenon have been questioned by some, considering that as women in Iran, people might have to face many obstacles, will be forced to be veiled, and will become victims of prejudice in a society with established laws against women.

Theoretical Framework: Understanding gender in and through psychoanalysis

Psychoanalysis, as a tradition, has tended to understand gender dysphoria as an issue which stemmed from arrested development, with some difficulties revolving around drive management, relaxing bisexuality fantasies, and shaky object relations in early life (Stoller, 1968). In line with most early conceptualizations and treatments of homosexuality, the ideal treatment considered for gender dysphoria was organized around resolving conflicts of that sort so that an individual's believed gender would be in concert with their physical outlook, which was believed as inflexible and impossible to change (Socarides, 1970; Meyer, 1982; Oppenheimer, 1991; Parfitt, 2007).

Psychoanalytic theory of gender is now broadening its understanding of gender, sexual orientation and the body as a gendered phenomenon: in other words, contemporary psychoanalytic theory is aiming to understand how the body meets gender. So, these recent trends consider psychoanalysis and surgery as "not necessarily mutually exclusive" (Winograd, 2014, p. 58). In a rather bold turn which echoes some of the developments in recent theorizing, Harris (1996) proposes that it is actually quite more plausible to regard gender dysphoria as "gender dysphorias in the parents and family, often expressed in the unconscious wishes and needs of the adults in the family system, played out in the meanings they assign and perceive in the child's gender" (p. 366). It is important to note that she regards genderedness as "not an identity by default" which seems radically different from those who take gender as a granted given. Though we should not be ignorant of the suffering of our patients, we should also be well aware that those who complete a transsexual transition

> [A]re very often disappointed with the results, suggesting that the belief that changing genders will make everything "all right" is based on a kind of magical thinking that tries to simplify more complicated problems of identity (Wingorad, 2014, p. 61).

This is shown in the narratives presented in this paper: the ultimate search for the perfect and magical penis or vagina. Most analysts, however, prefer to stay silent in relation to their views on other forms of sexualities besides heterosexuality (Lemma, 2013). The reluctance to do so may stem from an anxiety that revolves around political correctness. One might also speculate that a fear of "coming out", and holding a position that non-heterosexual sexualities are not necessarily pathological, may "expose the analyst to the charge that they are not in touch with the 'facts of life'" (Lemma, 2012, p. 267). Most of the theorizing traditions aiming to grasp the issue of transsexuality often conceptualized it as if it were a monolithic construct, associated with a homogeneous group of individuals (Lemma, 2012). Having the idea of plural transsexualities in mind, Lemma (2013, 2012) identifies two themes in her work with transsexual patients. The first theme to emerge is concerned with what her patients "variously called a 'gap', 'disjoin' or 'incongruity' between the given body and the body they identify as their 'true' physical home (Lemma, 2013, p. 278). The second theme revolves around how the self is being visually perceived and how it is experienced as a visual object. In this regard, the transsexual experience is indeed to be found as rooted in the visual order. As their non-conforming outlook calls on the *gaze* of the other inescapably, thus they "inhabit an internal *and* external scopic economy" (Lemma, 2013, p. 278). According to Lemma we could claim that repeated hindrance of embodiment along with the absence of the receptive mind of an other who is capable of "giving meaning, that is 'naming', the baby's sensory and motor experiences from when he 'wakes up' to the external world" (Lemma, 2012, p. 264), and engages with it might be one of the pathways to transsexuality, and cause a serious incongruence between the subjective experience and the given body because there is no mentalization of the bodily experience (Gergely & Uroka, 2008). Despite the 'democratization of transgenderism' (Gherovici, 2010), we should keep in mind that this 'new' body is *always* and inevitably a reconstructed and modified body which has its own unique history (Lemma, 2013). As a result, negotiation with this disloyal and treacherous internal history is crucial in post-operative adjustment. All this makes it necessary to create a space for listening to the experience of the transsexual individual, a space between previous trends of "pathologizing and politicizing" (Lemma, 2012, p. 267).

While many contemporary psychoanalytic authors seem to have taken the oath of analytic neutrality and agreed that as a tool, it "allows us to unveil, enter contact with and give voice to all parts of our patient" (Eizirik, p. xxi in Ambrosio, 2009), but in this case, the patient is taken to be a *known object*. Treating transsexuality as such reveals the authors' wish for conformity, unity and omnipotence when facing the enigma of sexuality. Pathologizing transsexuality might proceed from tremendous anxiety provoked by the fantasy of the transsexual who's a detriment on "nature and transgresses the law" (Gozlan, 2014, p. 3).

This insight, Freudian in origin, that our sexuality is utterly run by the primary process means that the psyche is mostly stamped not by categorical opposition, but by difference (Bass, 2006). Understanding castration as a response to anxiety allows one to consider it not as an event, but as a fantasy that tries to conceal the very essence of difference, by presupposing that what is absent was present once upon a time. In other words, gender identity is a form of splitting that does what it can to blind us to the obscurity of the unknown of desire. In this regard, the concept of transsexuality speaks out about "this inherent tension of the enigma as a representation both of a desire for completion and its impossibility" (Gozlan, 2013, p. 6). Again, the anxiety that the transsexual body evokes points to a breakdown in the defensive interplay between gender and sexuality that serves as a mask for uncertainty.

Reading the work of Gozlan (2014), we are offered a chance to let go of common, assumed meanings and regard transsexuality as an "object of phantasy," "an object through which the void of selfhood and desire materializes itself" (p. 14). Appreciating Lacan's concept of an Act, Gozlan puts a major question forward: "Can a subject survive her or his history?" (p. 42). He sheds light on an uncertain, precarious line between reality and phantasy, emphasizing on "sublimation as a phantastical bridge between language and the body" (p. 42) and when confronted by fearful, jumpy pathologization of others, he stands for a view in which the transsexual renders his/her body a piece of art and declairs their inner identity to be an object of aesthetic. "Gozlan identifies a psychic transition from medicalization to embodiment" (Molofsky, 2015). This view causes transsexuality to be considered as a psychic position in its own right, capable of facing this essentially paradoxical experience of transition and the valence of phantasy and affect that accompany such aesthetic conflicts over the nature of beauty and being.

Attempting to move from the traditional hetero-normative approach of psychoanalysis, Charles Shepherdson (2000) builds his statements using Catherine Millot's work to articulate the body as being irreducible to either "a natural fact nor a cultural construction" (p. 94). Millot (1990) claimed that any sort of modification of genitals by means of SRS was precarious and likely to fail, as no change in the anatomy can for sure afford a fantastic position beyond lack and desire.

Another noteworthy issue when dealing with transsexuality is "the wish to correct the 'error of nature'" (Gherovici, 2011). Here, the person relinquishes a distorted, fallacious sexual narrative which accepts the phallus as a signifier that would define sexual difference. When this sexual discourse based on phallic monism is taken away and done with, the error is no longer a matter of the symbolic order, but that of nature and hence, to be resolved there in the real. Usually, the wish for sexual reassignment is aimed at rewriting the error in the symbolic register by fixing it in the body as realm of the real. But the paradox is that something is always lacking in human sexuality, something is always wrong as human sexuality is doubtfully defined by means of an organ that plays the role of a signifying instrument.

Here, following Gherovici (Gherovici, 2011) we ought to remember Lacan's dictum that 'there is no sexual relation', which is a way of saying that the unconscious knows no female sex; the unconscious is ignorant of the two sexes and, in fact, is a monosexual or, one could say, homosexual entity which recognizes only one signifier for both sexes: the phallus. The phallus deals with phallic jouissance, though there's no doubt that there exist other forms of jouissance which are not necessarily phallic; even though they're not included in the arena of signifiers. So, sexual positioning is situated on an erroneous basis that takes the real organ, in flesh and blood, as a defining sign of sexual difference. The corrective statement made by some transsexuals might be revolving this common error after all: "If you think that because I have a penis I am a man, that is an error; I can be a woman who has a penis." Or conversely, "If you think that not having a penis makes me a woman, this is an error because I am a man without a penis" (Morel, 2000, p. 186). As the unconscious may recognize somebody with a penis as a woman or someone without a penis as a man, then in that sense, these narratives are absolutely right. Sexual positioning is not based on organ attribution and the transgender phenomenon testifies to the idea that there is nothing natural that would direct us to the opposite sex (Gherovici, 2011). The question of identity in the sphere of sexuality then comes to be a matter of secondary priority. As the unconscious does not portray masculinity or femininity as separate realms, there's no way to be sure about being a man or a woman: we have but a delightful uncertainty and that's all we could be sure about.

Gherovici (2011) ends her discussion by asking a last question. This last century witnessed an evolution of sex change technologies, but they have now spread so far as to create a discourse which bears marks of an essentialist identity per se. Intervening with one's sexual biology has made choice of one's gender an available option on demand. However, the introduction and development of such technologies that allow people to walk more easily over the sexual continuum have put the spotlight on an often unanswered question: "What makes a man a man and a woman a woman?" (Gherovici, 2011, p. 15). This we clearly see in the clinical material and narratives presented in this paper.

In Gherovici's (2010) words, "Fundamentally, bisexuality is not a 'third kind' of sexual identity that would stand between or beyond homosexuality and heterosexuality. On the contrary, it is something that puts in question the very concept of a symmetrical notion of sexual identity" (p. 77). Most fundamentally, Gherovici provides us with a theory of sexual difference, in general, and sexual difference, in particular, that dismisses the tradition of pathologization of transgenderism. In contrast to Judith Butler's view that "sex" is a normative construct, "forcibly materialized through time" (Butler, 1993, p. 1), which endows some bodies with cultural plausibility and regards some others as being "unthinkable" (p. xi), Gherovici claims that there is an unthinkable element about everybody and that "sexual difference names that unthinkable" (Carlson, 2016, p. 242).

Who is a real man? Who is a real woman? And why would holding that knowledge be a desirable outcome? What about at-times man, at-times woman, at-times everything in regards to this magical space of "in-between-ness", in this space between hiding and revealing?

It seems that within today's zeitgeist, in order for anything to be legitimate it has to be transparent, but transparency is the death of desire. We need to take back our secrets. This universal right of hiding and revealing, this Freudian game of Fort/Da (hide and seek; *cache-cache*) is being taken away from us in this corrupt culture of the primacy of transparency, where, supposedly, nothing is left to be revealed.

I know everything about you and you know everything about me, we are one and the same. If you claim to be a man, then be a man; get a penis, marry a woman and adopt a child; that is a photo I have a ready-made frame for in the closet of my mind. If you claim to be a woman, then get a vagina, live up to my very concrete definition of who a woman is. In order for you to be legitimate, I need to know what is it that you carry in your undergarments. I need to know and to see it: no secrets, no gender performative plays. *Be like others.*

Within this discourse there is no access to fantasy or symbolic communications, no possibilities of becomings, of secrets, of delightful uncertainties. This, then, is the death of desire, the death of the subject. We are told that societies and subjects must be transparent in order to be legitimate; this for psychoanalysis has to run contrary to anything that is creative and sublimatory, which has to be marginalized.

Is it not also true that within the discourse of transgenderity one also hears this limiting fantasy of transparency?

Psychoanalytic approaches to transgenderity

Following this contextualization and investigation of the current theoretical framework, three types of narratives will now be provided:

Narrative #1: Extracts from a long-term report by a supervisee, regarding a psychoanalytically oriented group he runs for Trans people.

Narrative #2: Transcripts from two documentaries
Narrative #3: Various direct interviews

Narrative #1 Extracts from a long-term report by a supervisee, regarding a psychoanalytically oriented group he runs for Trans people

I have had a psychoanalytically-oriented therapist in supervision with me for many years: he started a group to which attendance was obligatory in order to gain permission for surgery, at the university where he works in a very religious city in Iran. Here are samples of what he reported to me:

The group began with almost 15 members. It was quite predictable that the group would start with negative transference towards the therapy team and the judicial system.

In the first few sessions the discussions focused around explaining the reason why they were attending meetings that they considered as futile.

They said "We are only here to get justification for our surgery!"

After this first 'denial and confusion' phase the patients moved to the bargaining phase. For example they would say "Why don't you give us the confirmation letters for our operations, please! And after that we promise to attend group therapy for ten years!"

A sort of concreteness and lack of symbolization was observable among all the members, along with a great deal of acting out in the sessions. Generally the therapist did not feel they were doing any group work. It was more similar to a number of individuals talking separately without listening to each other. However, their impulsivity and action-orientedness lessened, and was managed gradually, by simultaneously both containing and confronting it.

Gradually their actions were transformed into verbal communications, such as expressions of anger towards authorities, their families and even towards their peers.

Within the next phase of the group, conversations turned to the concepts of masculinity and femininity. There were very concrete and stereotyped imaginary pictures about these two concepts. The therapist tried to deconstruct sexual and gender clichés by challenging and interpreting them as they appeared within the group dynamics and in the transference.

For example, they would say to him "...like you as a straight man" and the therapist would respond "Who knows?" Or when they mentioned some examples of gender-specific jobs, conducts or customs, he asked them if they all agreed with those fixed definitions.

It turned out that they had a large amount of information about their issues and their status as LGBT (lesbian, gay, bisexual, transgender) people. Some of them complained that god had created them like this and often expressed anger with the therapist along the lines of "Why should I be here? I am not mentally ill and don't need to be here!" But gradually they talked about their concerns and anxieties, such as their uncertainty about whether they are homosexual or transsexual. It should be noted that this concern was more common among F-to-M patients.

As the supervisor, I think that this becomes particularly problematic in a country like Iran, with a clear law against homosexuality which prescribes the death penalty as punishment.

Another source of serious anxiety among them was worry about the outcome of the surgery and whether the transgender operation would be successful (by that they meant a "great penis" or a "perfect vagina") or the operation would result in a botched catastrophe. Whether, in other words, their genitals would be good, functional and potent enough, or if they would result in a scandal for them within their relationships. Although it is interesting to note that these kinds of issues were more frequent among male-to-female patients, as they worried about the constructed vagina and whether it would have enough space and elasticity for a deep penetration, or would result in a bad, synthetic impression of labia. Female-to-male patients also had such concerns about the size and especially about the erection of the transplanted penis. However, they said that they could already satisfy their partners without a penis as women are often sensitive to being touched affectionately. Even the female-to-male members said that as they had "feminine hearts and masculine minds" they could understand women's feelings deeply, and were more empathic than straight men in relationships with them!

The members gradually talked more about their personal life and relationships. One male-to-female member said "I can't do the operation as long as my mom is alive, as she is old and sick, and she cannot tolerate this about me. After my operation I'll leave here and live with a new identity in another city. Nobody will recognize me after that." However, in a more recent session he said "I had never thought I might be able to accept my new identity as a transsexual in this society, but now after these sessions and after listening to others I feel I can stay, live and work here in my city: there is no reason to run away."

In some other sessions male-to-female members said: "Most of the other transsexuals who want to change their sexual identity are actually looking for a promiscuous life, like dirty rubbish. They have made a bad name for us and are responsible for the social stigma about Trans people in Iran."

This conversation led to a great deal of tension within the group.

They also had one session with the presence of their partners that was reported to me thusly:

It was interesting that all the partners that showed up were females (partners of F-to-M members). Discussing their feelings about having a female-to-male partner, it seemed that they were OK with their choices and had accepted the partners as 'real' men. However, they complained about their partners' lack of confidence in their sexual potency and identity as a real and original man, saying "They don't consider themselves 'real men' as much as we do!" One said: "There are so many people with a penis but they are not real men, however my partner is a real man for me although he has no penis! Because primarily I communicate with his internal world, feelings and soul!"

The therapist wondered in supervision why male-to-female members' partners had not come with them, because he had on many occasions previously noticed that those of female-to-male members were waiting for them at the end of the session in the waiting room.

An explanation about this may be strong sexist views, in which changing from a male to a female is considered as downgrading to a lower sex while changing from a female to a male is considered an upgrade to a higher sex, and this may be the reason why male-to-female members' partners are not willing to accompany them in the sessions. And perhaps because of this reason, male-to-female patients generally are more fragile and vulnerable, face more problems in their families, and social situations such as rejection and humiliation, as their condition raises severe castration anxieties in others.

There was a constant fear about not being accepted as a 'real' man or a 'real' woman. They negated and refused every sign of the opposite gender in an exaggerated way. One female-to-male patient once said "I don't talk on my mobile in a taxi as my voice is not manly enough!" And he insisted on wearing only what were — according to him — clearly masculine colors.

As we will continue to see within the other narratives reported below, there is a clear sense of "gender certainty" with these individuals.

As the group progressed, the members became more symbolic and abstract in their discourses. In one of the recent sessions, one of the F-to-M members who had been highly resistant and had a strong defense against the group, and was very silent in the beginning, reported the following.

"You remember how I was in a hurry, and insistent on having the operation as soon as possible! But it is strange: now that everything is ready for the surgery I feel neutral, and I'm not as delighted as I expected myself to be. I have questions and concerns now regarding the surgery that I would like to explore. Maybe I will still do it, but I want more time to think about it." "What are your concerns?" asked the therapist. He replied: "After a lot of arguments with my mother, she consented to my surgery, but these days when she looks at me I see a great regret in her eyes. I have three sisters, and you know like many other mothers she had always wished for a 'real original boy', not a fake, synthetic one! I feel guilty and worthless. All I will be, at most, will be a Pinocchio for her."

When the therapist asked the group what their thoughts were on this matter, they all agreed with the member, and it was revealed that there were similar concerns among the rest.

Another female-to-male member said:

"Now, before the surgery, we are prominent and attractive tomboys among the other females, but after the surgery our rivals will be straight men who are often stronger, more handsome and have better situations at work and in life: so we will fade away among real men!". And it was interesting that the same was true about M-to-F members, they also said "Now, in comparison with other men we are very cute and pretty 'she-males', but after the surgery, we will have to compete with 'original' females with more attractive and curved feminine bodies and soft feminine voices, and this makes it so difficult for us to get men's attention, in competition with 'original' girls."

All over the discourse we hear 'real' vs 'fake', 'original' vs 'copy', and discussion of 'perfect' vaginas and penises. In supervision the therapist told me one day "You know, after these groups I am really feeling castrated as a straight man. I do not live up to their ideals of what a man should be like. I always leave the groups feeling depressed and humiliated." I thought these were interesting counter-transference feelings. My own associations take me to Kiarostami's movie *Certified Copy*, and the metaphor of Pinocchio remains with me.

As the group progressed we did indeed see the opening of a mental space for ambiguity, with less concreteness and more ambivalence, more deconstruction, less certainty about getting the surgery: however this did not happen with every single member of the group. They were a few who, even though they were becoming much more able to mentalize their experience and symbolize their feelings, were still adamant about getting the surgery.

Of course, we are not suggesting that the creation of a space to talk should be with the intention of discouraging people from surgery. As the therapist reported to me "It does not matter if they get the surgery or not, but it is important that they think about why they want to do it and have a safe space to discuss and elaborate such a significant decision in their lives over a long period of time."

Narrative #2: Short Vignettes from two Documentaries

Heydar, a female-to-male trans person, always felt different from other girls. While with his family, he wore men's clothes and refused to wear a scarf. But Leila, who was a boy and a male-to-female trans person, has a different story: she grew up in a very traditional and patriarchal Azeri family. As a boy, she was very feminine and was always bullied at school. It was only after she got married that her family accepted her decision. Now, much later, Heydar and Leila are happily married. They have recently visited an orphanage in their area and hope to be recognized as eligible to adopt a child. Today their dreams are simple, and they don't feel different as a married couple now that their families accept them (excerpt from a report by Pikulicka-Wilczewska, A., 2015).

Expectations of the West can be exaggerated, as Shiva, a male-to-female transsexual who moved from Iran to Norway, reports:

> And about Norway, I thought they'd be more liberal. Most Norwegian lesbians, gays and transsexuals are expelled from their homes by their families. Just like in Iran... They tell them to go and they do. We're not accepted anywhere in the world. Our societies don't let us in easily. We're obliged to stay together. Many Norwegians, foreigners or especially Muslims... I ran away from that culture: the system, discrimination, male dominance, religion, God, 'haraam' and... and I was tortured and hurt. Then I found the same thing here. It is difficult to live the way you want. I'm doing it but it is difficult... really difficult and sometimes, it's dangerous. After the transition, I came to know Angelika as a woman who loved me as a woman. I walked in the street alongside her with pride. I felt wonderful and in my heart, ask those people in my past: where are you now? I wanted them to see this scene that I'm in now, because I'm with my preferred gender and with the person I love. Today, I have won and you have lost. (*Shiva: The Story of a Transsexual*, 2013).

In a documentary broadcast on the Islamic Republic's national television station, a female-to-male trans person reports: "I remember when they bought a pair of earrings for me and how I was disgusted by them."

Why such a strong, intense reaction to the other sex? Why be disgusted with earrings?

Another female-to-male subject states: "It is very important that people recognize the difference between a transsexual and a homosexual. Maybe we could consider transsexuality as a disorder, but it's not the same with homosexuality. My transsexuality's been approved by four sexologists. I just want to ask religious families to reduce and let go of their anxieties. There's a Fatwa in support of sex reassignment surgery. There's nothing to worry about."

Yet another female-to-male transsexual says: "We have Imam Khomeini's Fatwa. This is very important, at least for religious families. I informed my family, using Imam's Fatwa. I told them that I'm acceptable in the eyes of my religion. I'm also legally accepted. So I can be accepted by my family and in society. We transsexuals are newborns. I'm just one year old, and I will find the right place for me, and will get better each day." It seems that the support of family post-operation makes a significant difference in how things proceed. (IRIB, December 25th, 2015).

Narrative #3: Short Vignettes from Various Interviews

Could you describe the procedure you took for the surgery?

I went to a psychiatrist and passed five psychological exams. There were tests with answer sheets as well as pictures that I had to speak about. The questionnaires have a lie detector scale and you cannot lie. If you lie, they can catch you red-handed and sue you. Many people claim to be transsexuals to be exempted from military service, but they can't pass the tests.

Have you ever wanted to marry?

I had four suitors but as I cannot bear children, it ended nowhere. But after my surgery I will be able to have kids [sic]. I should say that we're very attractive to straight men and this attraction is becoming greater as time passes. But no man would stay in our lives. There are exceptions who are married, but they are exceptions. We need to culturally accept the marriage between straights and transsexuals. I consider transgenderity as the 'better' gender. It has the masculine attractions along with female delicacies. Transsexuality is a third sexuality.

Does it not mean that trans people don't have any particular identity?

No. transsexuality is a third sexuality. We should be in a situation where our kids read in their schoolbooks that we have men, women, transsexuals and androgynous people. We're not androgynous and hence you cannot say we don't have any particular identity.

(*The Boy who Became a Woman After 23 Years!*, 2015; Taraneh Aram, 2016)
This is interesting. Note this statement: "transsexuality is a third sexuality" from the same woman who, two paragraphs earlier, has said that after her surgery, she can have a child.

> A homosexual needs help to let go of this deviation. But a transsexual needs to undergo an SRS. We're not homosexuals. I hate homosexuals. I could have lived with a man in Europe or in the U.S. but I chose the surgery, with all its difficulties, in order to be a woman instead. (Interview with Taraneh Aram., February 20th, 2013)

There is a clear rejection of homosexuality, while transgenderity is authorized under the religious Fatwa. This produces a very particular situation in Iran. Transgenderity is legitimate but homosexuality gets the death penalty.

Another documentary, titled *Be Like Others* (2008), deals with the topic of transsexuality and transsexual issues in Iran.

The father of Ali, a trans person, (Ali is in fact Anoush's boyfriend/husband-to-be) takes the following view:

> "You just need to walk with him in the street to see what I mean. Almost everybody will turn around and say something. You can hear them saying: "he's gay" or stuff like that. I really think things will be much easier after his surgery. Now that he walks around in a woman's outfit, I can more easily get myself to think that he's a girl. It facilitates my relationship with him. And he has legal rights as well in this country. They used to pick on him before. And I was under pressure from people around me. Things will be better after his operation."

Then we meet Cleric Karaminia, a religious legislative authority on sex change operations, who preaches:

> "We're not talking about homosexuals here. They're doing something immoral… something against the religion. But for the ones who suffer from TS conditions, Islam offers a cure." The cleric also spoke at a conference in the city of Gorgan in the north of Iran where, among many others, Anoush and his mother were present.

> Cleric Karaminia continues: "As Imam Khomeini noted, sex reassignment surgery is not *haraam* [religiously wrong]. As he said, every deed is possible, unless it is strictly spoken against in the Quran, or the Hadith announces it as a sin. Secondly, if changing one's gender could be a sin because it modifies divine creation, then almost everything we do would be religiously wrong because we're constantly making changes in divine creation."

Anoush asks him: "I'm more confident in a female costume. I'm usually harassed when in a man's outfit. Why shouldn't I wear it before my operation?"

He replies: "In the past, there used to be people who'd dress as a member of the opposite sex, which is totally against Sharia. It's against the proper morals and disrupts social order".

It should be noted that there is actually quite a lot of pressure to have the surgery from the government in Iran: then things are considered clear, with no ambiguity. We meet Farhad, Aliasghar's childhood friend who has come from his village to be with Aliasghar during his operation. Farhad is also thinking about a possible course of surgery. When confronted by the reporter about wearing female costume while still a male, Farhad replies: "Why I should be forced to have surgery? What if this surgery is harmful to my body?" The reporter responds: "If you want to stay a man and still wear female clothes, then you're not a transsexual, you're a transvestite ... or maybe a homosexual. You should make up your mind. You're either a woman or a man."

Farhad: "Then if I want to live, I'm obliged to succumb to your non-ambiguous condition."
The reporter: "I suspect that you want to have it both ways."
Farhad: "What do you think leads these people to come here and ask to be a man or woman?"
The reporter: "So you mean transsexuals shouldn't change their bodies and just need to change clothes?"
Farhad: "I'm just saying that this obligation leaves no room for a choice. That 'obligation' comes from you and people like you."
The Reporter: "So you are not contemplating surgery?"
Farhad: "What do you mean by that? I'm forced to undergo the surgery. Society forces me to do so. I'm obliged to go with surgery because my family wouldn't accept me this way. I'm an Iranian and want to live in Iran. They've told me that I *must* either be a woman or a man."
The Reporter: "So you decided to be a woman."
Farhad: "No, I didn't. There is no decision. Society has forced me to."

This is a perfect example of pattern #1. Be like the others. Be a man or a woman. It is true we see it in an exaggerated form in Iran. But I wonder about the universality of this politics of sameness. Could it be that because of the particular situation in Iran we see an exaggerated symptom of the larger disease, of a universal psychoanalytic politics of sameness?

Aliasghar is admitted to the hospital and is having surgery in one day's time. He says:

If you want to know your identity, you should undergo the operation. This is what god has done. I've heard in other counties men can marry each other but what's the use of it? Anal sex is a big sin. Here, I don't have the right to work, nor to live. If I went to a male dominant environment, I'd be molested. They'd make fun of me. I can't go to work in a female environment because I don't have any identity. But after surgery, everything will be fine, as it must be. You will be identified. *But if I was not in Iran, I wouldn't have the surgery.* I don't know what they do in foreign countries. I've just heard they have their own rights. But if I was not obliged, I wouldn't have agreed to the operation. I wouldn't have messed with god's creation. [My emphasis]

Farhad speaks as he's beside Aliasghar's bed: "…I once spoke with an authority about my concerns. I told him that I'm a Muslim and Islam is a religion of reason. There should be a plan for my life. What'd happen to me if they'd just perform an operation on me and *disfigure my body* and then dump me in the street? It'd lead to social corruption. That's what's going to happen if they leave me be, no? … *If I were not in Iran, I wouldn't choose the surgery* … I swear to god, it's mostly what happens after the surgery that upsets me most." [My emphasis]

Aliasghar (after the operation): "*I'm in pain, just like a woman in labor. It is not worth it.*" [My emphasis]

One year later, Farhad, who came to support Aliasghar during his surgery, has left village life for Tehran. Though he contemplated having SRS, he's now changed his mind after seeing what this did to his friend's body:

When I came to Tehran, I got to know people who had surgery five, six, even ten years ago. I got to know more about their lives. Some committed suicide because they could not be satisfied sexually. They lost a lot, and the side effects would appear gradually. I just wanted to have a decent life, like everybody else. When I saw all this, I decided to postpone the surgery. I didn't want my life to be worse than what it was. In Tehran, I saw what happens with my own eyes. No one told me anything. I witnessed it myself. I think god favors me, that he led me to come here and see these things for myself. I then realized it'd be a big mistake if I had the surgery.

In response to the suggestion that it would make things easier if he had the surgery, Farhad replies: "But what's the price? To disfigure my body? Why should I go with a surgery after which I'd need to succumb to doing things I don't like to… what's the use of it?"

Conclusion: From a Politics of Transparency towards an Ethics of Ambiguity. In praise of Ambiguity, of Difference and of Inbetween-ness

'Greet yourself in your thousand other forms' (Hafez)

At times I believe that within this new and trendy politically correct psychoanalytic discourse of transgenderity, we are still practicing a new variation of the same old limiting, heteronormative view of familiarity; naming and categorizing trans-embodiments within the same framework. A clear example of this becomes evident within Iranian Sharia law which prescribes that if you want to be with men, you must become a woman, so that you can be digested into a limited view of human gender and sexuality. Analysts can thus also escape from having to deal with anxieties of their own regarding the gender fluidity of every human being. But this politically correct discourse imprisons us within a boring and concrete way of being, and takes away any possibilities of *becomings* that are always in flux, always changing.

Let me clarify that I do not think it is the job of the analyst to tell someone to get sex reassignment surgery or not: this is a decision that the person should make for themselves. In this, it is similar to any other decision, but at the same time we cannot escape the fact that something drastic is being done to the body.

As with every significant decision that is brought up in analysis, time and space should be dedicated to the person, in an attempt to develop fantasies, symbolizations and dreams, freedom and transformations, sublimations and becomings away from the concreteness of having to choose one's gender identifications according to one's sexual organ.

In this specific case of trans-embodiments, a great number of questions remain: why has there been such a rise in surgeries? Why is there a high suicide rate in some countries after the surgery? Why do we categorize all transsexuals and transgender people under the same labels, (i.e 'they are all psychotics', or 'none of them are psychotics') when what we really need is to 'open up the roof', as Iranian poet Hafez advised us in the fourteenth century?

Should the fact that in the final analysis something drastic is being done to the body be elaborated and addressed, or should we hide our own anxieties regarding any sort of fluidity, unfamiliarity and difference under the facade of political correctness?

This is not psychoanalysis: psychoanalysis has never been about being politically correct, it is a subversive discourse and it must remain such.

This does not mean that we should not acknowledge the fact that for years psychoanalytic theory has been imposing a heteronormative discourse upon trans-embodiments.

In this paper, I have attempted to show that some, though by no means all, contemporary psychoanalysts have been hiding their same old gender and sexual anxieties under this new politically correct discourse. It is still a heteronormative, binary discourse of sameness and naming, that of categorizing. I would go as far as saying that this is now even more dangerous than before, as there is no possibility of analyzing the issue.

Everybody is so 'nice': what can we say? This is the problem with a politically correct discourse. It is a closed loop, or an echo chamber.

I invite you to a carnival of masks. This is a community of subjects hospitable towards themselves, the other, and the other within themselves, in the name of a politics of unfamiliarity, of ambiguity, and of *becomings*. We need to be hospitable to this playground of monsters, of zombies: we need to awaken our spirits, our witches and sorcerers. And yes, for a while it will be scary. We will be dizzy. We will lose all our imaginary weapons: but I am convinced that this is the only way to do justice to our debt towards our desirous selves.

I encourage you to join me in this playground of monsters, in awakening the spirits of the underworld, of the unconscious, towards a discourse of desire narrated within and beyond one thousand and one tales.

This paper concludes with a poem by Hafez, our celebrated poet from Shiraz, which I find speaks to this topic.

All the Hemispheres

Leave the familiar for a while
...
Open up the Roof
...
Change rooms in your mind for a day
...
Greet Yourself
In your thousand other forms
As you mount the hidden tide and travel back home

Bibliography

Adrienne Harris, 'Animated conversation: Embodying and gendering', Gender and Psychoanalysis, 1 (1996), 361–383.

Agnès Oppenheimer, 'The wish for a sex change: A challenge to psychoanalysis?', The International Journal of Psychoanalysis, 72 (1991), 221–231.

Alan Bass, *Interpretation and Difference: The Strangeness of Care* (Palo Alto, CA: Stanford University Press, 2006).

Alessandra Lemma, 'Research off the couch: Re-visiting the transsexual conundrum', Psychoanalytic Psychotherapy, 26, 4 (2012), 263–281.

— —, 'The body one has and the body one is: Understanding the transsexual's need to be seen', The International Journal of Psychoanalysis, 94, 2 (2013), 277–292.

Anthony Parfitt, 'Fetishism, transgenderism and the concept of "castration"', Psychoanalytic Psychotherapy, 21 (2007), 61–89.

Catherine Millot, *Horsexe: Essays on Transsexualism*, trans. by Kenneth Hylton (New York: Autonomedia, 1990).

Charles Shepherdson, *Vital Signs: Nature, Culture, Psychoanalysis* (New York: Routledge, 2000).

Charles Socarides, 'A psychoanalytic study of the desire for sexual transformation ('transsexualism'): The Plaster-of-Paris man', International Journal of Psychoanalysis, 51, 3 (1970), 341–349.

Colette Chiland, *Transsexualism*, trans. by Philip Slotkin (Middletown, CT: Wesleyan University Press, 2003).

Genevieve Morel, *Ambigüedadessexuales: Sexuación y psicosis* (Buenos Aires: Manantial, 2000).

Gérard Wajcman, 'Exposed Intimacy, Extorted Intimacy', Symptom, 29 May 2012, http://www.lacan.com/symptom13/?p=66.

Giovanna Ambrosio and others, *Transvestism, Transsexualism in the Psychoanalytic Dimension*, ed. by Giovanna Ambrosio (London: Karnac, 2009).

György Gergely, and Zsolt Uroka, 'Attachment, affect-regulation and mentalization: The developmental origins of the representational affective self', in *Social Cognition and Developmental Psychopathology*, ed. by Carla Sharp, Peter Fonagy, and Ian Goodyer (Oxford: Oxford University Press, 2009), pp. 305–342.

Iranian Legal Medicine Organization (ILMO), *Statistical yearbook of legal medicine 2006 till 2010* / Saalnaameye Pezeshkiye Qanuniye Iran, 1385 taa 1389 (Tehran: ILMO, 2011).

Jon Meyer, 'The theory of gender identity disorders', Journal of the American Psychoanalytic Association, 30 (1982), 381–418.

Judith Butler, *Bodies That Matter: On the Discursive Limits of Sex* (Abingdon, Oxon, NY: Routledge, 2011).

Kirsten Dahl, 'Fantasies of gender', The Psychoanalytic Study of the Child, 43 (1988), 351–365.

Merle Molofsky, review of *Transsexuality and the Art of Transitioning: A Lacanian Approach*, by Oren Gozlan, Psychoanalytic Review, 102, 3 (2015), 423–426.

Oren Gozlan, *Transsexuality and the Art of Transitioning: A Lacanian approach* (London: Routledge, 2014).

— —, 'Transsexuality As a State of Mind: Commentary on "A Matter of Choice", by Jean Wolff Bernstein (DIVISION/Review, 3, Fall 2011, pp. 4–5), and "Which Side Are You On", by Richard Ruth and Helen Devinney (DIVISION/Review, 5, Summer 2012, pp. 12–14)', published on academia.edu, April 2013.

Patricia Elliot, 'A psychoanalytic reading of transsexual embodiment', Studies in Gender and Sexuality, 2 (2001), 295–325.

Patricia Gherovici, *Please Select your Gender: From the invention of hysteria to the democratising of transgenderism* (New York: Routledge, 2010).

— —, 'Psychoanalysis needs a sex change', Gay and Lesbian Issues and Psychology Review, 7, 1 (2011), 3–18.

Robert Jesse Stoller, 'A further contribution to the study of gender identity', International Journal of Psychoanalysis, 49 (1968), 364–368.

Shanna Carlson, '*Please Select your Gender: From the invention of hysteria to the democratizing of transgenderism* by Patricia Gherovici', The International Journal of Psychoanalysis, 97, 1 (2016), 241–245.

Sigmund Freud, 'Three essays on the theory of sexuality', in *The Standard Edition of the Complete Psychological Works of Sigmund Freud*, vii, ed. & trans. by James Strachey (London: Hogarth Press, 1905), pp. 123–246.

Wendy Winograd, 'The Wish to Be a Boy: Gender Dysphoria and Identity Confusion in a Self-Identified Transgender Adolescent', Psychoanalytic Social Work, 21, 1–2 (2014), 55–74.

Multimedia and online resources

Agnieszka Pikulicka-Wilczewska, 'Transsexuality in Iran: A liberal law in a conservative state', Middle East Eye, 30 November 2015, www.middleeasteye.net/in-depth/features/transsexuality-iran-liberal-law-conservative-state-1887443646.

Angus McDowall and Stephen Khan, 'Maryam Khatoon Molkara – The Ayatollah and the transsexual', Independent, 25 November 2004, www.independent.co.uk/news/world/middle-east/the-ayatollah-and-the-transsexual-21867.html.

'Interview with Taraneh Aram', 20 February 2013, https://www.youtube.com/watch?v=tNNnsqyOpIs.

IRIB (Islamic Republic of Iran Broadcasting), 'Documentary on transsexuality', Aparat, 25 December 2015, http://www.aparat.com/v/lJEc6.

Khabar Online. 'Every year, more than 270 Iranians undergo SRS / 56 percent want to be a woman / Saalaane Bish Az 270 Iraani Tagheire Jensiat Midahand / 56 Darsade Motaghaazian Mikhaahand Zan Baashand', Kabar Online, 3 December 2012, http://www.khabaronline.ir/detail/260988/society/health.

Robert Trait, 'A fatwa for freedom', Guardian, 27 July 2005, https://www.theguardian.com/world/2005/jul/27/gayrights.iran.

— —, 'Sex changes and a draconian legal code: gay life in Iran', Guardian, 25 December 2007, https://www.theguardian.com/world/2007/sep/25/iran.roberttait.

'Shiva: The Story of a Transsexual', You Tube, 26 December 2013, https://www.youtube.com/watch?v=ViJKS8jsuhY.

Tanaz Eshaghian, 'Be like others (Transsexuals in Iran) 2008', You Tube, 27 January 2016, https://www.youtube.com/watch?v=3rAaBJoOqpk.

'Taraneh Aram', You Tube, 8 January 2016, https://www.youtube.com/watch?v=A_nEejHsCRg.

'The boy who became a woman after 23 years!', You Tube, 6 Feburary 2015, https://www.youtube.com/watch?v=oBtHkDm5Y1w.

BODY'S POLYSEMY AND THE RECENT CHANGES IN THE HISTORY OF SENSITIVITY

Masculine, feminine and bisexual in today's world

MARCELO VIÑAR

My body remains silent only when I am not thinking about it. "Health is the silence of the organs", Virchow, (a pathologist), used to say, in the XIX century. Yet, its malfunction is strident. Beyond the alternation or the decisiveness of the physiological functions, when the body is aching or suffering, the soul is moaning and the body prevails. The mind gets imprisoned.

This is evident in the extreme experience of a serious disease or the one of torture. I have learned this in the hospital, back when I was a student, and later on while accompanying beloved people to die. I have learned it in literature too, within the universe of those who ended in concentration camps (Gil, Liscano, Antelme, Amery, Levi, Semprun). In those extreme conditions, the harmonic bond between the body and the conscious mind breaks and the unity splits in two. Affected by torture and disease, the body transforms into something else, a monster that challenges us and plagues us as an enemy from whom we cannot escape.

Moving from the monosemic and binary language of medicine and leaning towards the multifaceted polysemy of the Freudian language, it emerges that every morning we have a different awakening or, at least, one with more shades. It is just one moment, when the alarm clock is ringing, or in the shower and, before we even start thinking, our body informs us whether we are or not in a good disposition, or if we are crestfallen or disheartened. This moment of introspection is brief and discontinuous but frequent. Only in closeness we can notice its existence, since the body speaks to us in a very intimate language. I suppose that this personal experience is shared within the human beings, even if singularly for each one. Citing Freud from *Beyond the Pleasure Principle*: "the relation between pleasure and displeasure is the darkest and unfathomable sector of the emotional life".

Diametrically opposed to the painful experience is the extreme experience of pleasure: the moment where we fall in love. Another of those cases where the body becomes crucial (not as a fulminant disease or as torture, but with the perseverance of endless time) is when the sexual excitement throbs persistently and decisively. Perhaps the prime adolescence is the most accepted moment of this experience, yet I do not think it is ascribable to that age only.

There is a difference between when the desired or the attractive matches the accepted models and social conventions, that is, when it is in harmony with the hegemonic uses of a specific culture, and with when the object of the subject's desire collides with the cultural morality. In this case, the intimacy of the erotic feeling find itself overwhelmed by the view of the collective imagination. The duality created by the one who desires and his object of desire becomes ternary, pushed beyond the physical tension between the subject and his object of attraction. The subject of the conscience (which Freud called the clown of the triple slavery) find himself besieged and invaded from the official morality that interferes with the vicissitudes of desire and prohibition. During all the human history tensions existed, as well as assaults and clashes between those who fit the standard and those who find themselves outside of it, the dissidents and the heretics.

Nonetheless, in the last half of a century — just an instant in the enormity of human history — the sexualities that, until some decades ago, where considered aberrant and punishable, therefore clandestine, are, nowadays, characterized by a sort of pride that, sometimes, promotes exhibitionism. In the collective imagination of half of the planet, what once was despicable is now legit, also admirable, sometimes. It goes without saying that this appreciation is only applicable to the occidental sensibility of learned middle and high classes. In the other hemisphere people still stone sodomites and adulterous women. To enter the world of multiculturalism and the one of the marginalized sectors would mean a complexity that the limits of this essay could not confront, dealing with our area and social groups only.

In the confused waters of the modern liquidity is where our aim is set. The time where Freud's studies focused on curing the depraved has ended and the "politically correct" has performed a rotation of 180 degrees, proclaiming tolerance and the right to be different.

We no longer use strong walls to distinguish between what is normal and what is pathological, we no longer have those clear rules on the duality, that excluded "homosexual" from "heterosexual", conveying a strong model for describing sexuality. The sexual difference, postulated by Freud as the base for other differences, finds herself hit by the tsunami of changes, whose dimensions and outcome are still difficult to determine.

While the libertarian spirits are incline to legit the new sexualities, the religious and legal extremisms still keep on considering them as abnormalities to correct. The reaction to the scandal can be friendly or violent but it is present, in the collective psychology. I also ask myself whether the new sexuality signals an unprecedented reality or if it is a change in the visibility of facts that live, instead, from the dawn of time and whose relevancy originates from the progresses that were made in the medical fields of surgery and endocrinology. Technology and mentality that were once varied faces of the process of acknowledgement and of the coexistence codes, are today intertwined with interdependent determinations. The material modifications of the body that used to be possible only in daydreaming, are now defended as the right to health and helped by medical knowledge. The life and death of Michael Jackson is paradigmatic of this cosmic vision, as Dany Robert Dufour, and others, have said.

***

For psychoanalysis this is an unseen scenery. How could we define the specificity of our perspective? Which is the psychologic position in front of the extended range of the new sexualities? Is it a doctrinal position or a popular one? With which criteria should we divide the otherness to legalize and the one to fight?

We inherit from Freud the sacred vow of neutrality and abstinence, and it is a paradox, a contradiction, since the same Freud recognizes his limits and specifies the trouble in being completely neutral on decisive human issues. Clearly there is no moralism nor "everything works". Then, where do we position ourselves? How do we legitimize the specificity of the willing subject? And where do we place prohibition, that is an unavoidable dimension for the constitution of desire?

Moreover, obstinate and lasting complaints are there, as well as realities that bind body and soul in a stable and weighty way, intertwined and enigmatic, that psychopathology taught us to classify as hysteria, hypochondria or psychosomatic illness. Amidst of all of this we, in our profession, sail between knowledge and ignorance, with the ambition and the instruction to help our patient, make a living and enrich our reflections. Each one of us knows the percentage of these three parameters.

What interests me is to set as aleph (as the starting point) that the borders between the sensible and desiring meat and its arrest in the discourse is a nodal point of what we call the your-self. It is, as well, an essential point of attraction in the must do of psychoanalysis: one's own body as the muse of a multitude of metaphors.

I set position: biology and discourse are essential edges of the questioner and self-theorizing text. In my advice, these have to constitute a defining feature of the human condition, with as much or even more relevance than other traditional and less relevant (biologic) data. Freud defined this accurately and without doubt: the differences of sexes and generations are the coordinates where psychic structure places itself. These coordinates organize diversity and define the singularity that resides in each one of us. These foundations are the ones that are questioned in the contemporary reality.

Since theoretical discrepancies tend to reside more in the premises than in the development, I want to define my starting point as a place of conviction and controversy.

Biology and discourse tie in the body a specific reality that is not accessible when the two are isolated or when one of the two is awarded with supremacy on the other. For example, "Volver a los "17"" is a universal nostalgia that Violeta Parra immortalized in her song. It expresses, in a compact and eloquent way, the freshness of the prime of life, always seen as a great loss. However, the inescapable effect of chronological time in the psychic process is as specific as the shadows during dawn and dusk, in those who perceive themselves as blurry colours and shapes, difficult to distinguish in broad day as well as in the dark of nights. Gender and age are determining factors of identities dynamics.

***

It is worth relying on the reasoning of Anthropologist Francoise Héritier, which I am going to freely summarize as follows:

It is necessary:

a) Being careful not to overlap or mix up the act of conception and the one of filiation. Conception comes from a biological field and is characterized by its link with the body, whereas filiation comes from a symbolic field and derives from a social agreement between the subject and its culture. Keeping this heterogeneity in mind, I line up with the primacy and centrality of the social agreement of filiation over the act of conception, the latter being what biology and religion use to defend arguable certainties.

b) My second idea is that the exploration of the issue and the arguments cannot, and should not, aim to the certain truth of natural science or empirical science. It should, instead, preserve its conjectural identity and always be open to changes and controversy. Especially since its productiveness comes from its heuristic being and not from its demonstrative one.

c) The contemporary knowledge of the reproductive physiology allows to dissociate the erotic dimension of orgasm from the reproductive call that comes from the conservation of the species. The contemporary, civic and political debate concerning the voluntary termination of pregnancy should be included among the quandaries of New Parenting, as an act of choice and responsibility. Those who boast about the right of life of the embryo forget how damaging to the psyche could be an undesired or unexpected child.

d) Last but not least, Parenting and Filiations is an historic, cultural and anthropologic theme to which us psychoanalysts can contribute but we have to avoid the frequent indiscretion towards a boastful and truth lacking legislative position. As Piera Aulagnier says, we do not dispone of a sonography of the soul that allows to predict the equilibrium between the desire of having a child and the unconscious filiation impulses that are not disposable.

***

I do not really know where the intersection of the psychic structure's path and the history of sensibility's one places itself, but I do firmly think that these are intertwined parameters that do have influence one on the other.[1] Where are the ties between the most intimate of the cauldron of pulsation and what is accepted or rejected by the dominant beliefs of the culture in which we live?

Acceptancy or hate for the different dissolve both in the sexual register and in ethnic and religious racism. Why do we bind blacks, Jews and homosexuals together when there clearly is that much heterogeneity between them? Precisely because of this perplexity, I look to outline this problem. It is evident that the replacement of principles that occurred between the generations has created this crossroads. With this term we are carried to Delphi and to the crime of patricide. Without reaching that point, I name sensitivity's history that hegemonic collective imagination of an historic moment, which sets the boundary between the normal and the

---

1   To this, our permanent dialogue with the historians José Pedro Barrán and Gerardo Caetano has been decisive.

transgressor, the scared and the profane, the appealing and the repulsing. I cite Castoriadis's claim:

> Racism is involved with something way more universal than what is usually admitted. It is a particularly sharp and embittered sprout, the monstrous specification of a feature that is empirically verified as almost universal in the human societies. It deals with the inability to be one's self without excluding the other and the incapability to exclude the other without devaluating him or even hating him.

The stance of the singular subject in front of the prevailing imagination is nourished by interior ghosts, suggestions and commands that come from the *socius*, in magnitude and proportions that vary from one individual to the other. The beliefs are always a mixture between endo-psychic and transpersonal factors. Illustration does not free us that easily from the theory of the animal magnetism that preceded it. Even though the autonomy of a subject is difficult to measure, the daily experience and a shallow look to history shows us that there are some beings that are more suggestible than others. That is how diversity gets pictured as one of the most outstanding features of our species. The expectation of regularity from chance, in natural science, has been subverted in human science. Cultural ethnocentrism is also a powerful operator and a dangerous chute for cruelty and human destructiveness. In his book "Las Cacerías del Hombre" (LOM — Trilce Editores, 2014), Grégoire Chamayou provides an excellent historic summary of this wretched face of mankind.

Here is a shred of daily life to frame my consideration: a young and clearheaded colleague of mine, mother of three adolescent females, refers me some dialogues that she had with her daughters: "But, mom, you don't understand the difference between fucking and making love. You also ignore that in my class (the girls are about fifteen years old) the most popular are the bisexuals, that look down on hetero and homosexuals, because they are depriving themselves from half of the party".

Another example from the São Paulo colleague Susanna Muszkat: "A young man brings a baby girl to the paediatrician. The receptionist gathers the data until they arrive to the mother's name. The man answers: she does not have a mother, she has two fathers. The receptionist is unsettled but, after a moment of astonishment exclaims: that's nice!".

Explaining my answer or reaction: I do not believe I am strait-laced nor finicky, but my dignity of respectable elderly man is under siege. I evoke Freud's speech that claims that the difference between sexes and between generations is a foundation of the psychic architecture. I could have never talk, in my fifteens, in such a way with my parents and I would have condemned bisexuality even if, in the private confidentiality of my mind, no human or divine power could have had the power to impede me to play with multiple deprived fantasies. The contemporary contents might as well be the same ones of my youth but they are protected within the private enclosure of the unmentionable. Then it is not about the content of fantasy, but about the barter between the private and the displayable, up to the ostentation of the displayable, to the presence or absence of borders between what is public and what is private. That is what I claim as relevant. Perhaps there are no changes in the individual's interior but there are in his relations. An inversion between modesty and promiscuity might happen, and it might happen faster and faster every time.

What created social interaction in my generation was the issue of the Hombre Nuevo. And let's not talk about the ending of those ideals that tied up our millenarianism illusion and that are, nowadays, crumbling down. What is creating social interaction nowadays, in the groups of young people and with unusual vigor are the music genres, the excesses of drug addictions and the risky behaviors.

I understand that bringing up these topics out of a transference context might emerge as not much analytical and poorly fruitful. But only listening, in the confidential privacy of the meeting, stops us from examining the interactions between the psychic conflict and the social field.

***

Anatomy is destiny — this famous quote is attributed to both Freud and Napoleon — denounces in the collective imagination the certainty or the belief that biology has supremacy when it comes to defining the identity. With this premise, the normality of the heterosexual and the abnormality (or pathology) of the homosexual are easy to establish. More over there is the religious imperative commandment to the perpetuation of the species, that pushed the orgasmic function into a secondary, pleasant and sinful dimension. Those were passed times that we now view with contempt, a simple equation that has now broken into pieces. The sexual diversity (LGBT) moved from embarrassment to pride.

During the last half-century, a change in perspective was legitimized, and it included a modification of the current language (let us not mention the academic). Therefore, we no more say difference in sex but difference in gender. We no more say fellatio but we say oral sex and this is to underline the sociocultural constructive nature used to define the sexual differences.

In the time of my youth a prevailing homophobic collective imagination ruled, in scales that went from scorn and mockery as wide-spread aggressions to a radical sanction of sin and crime. The latter behavior is still current in half of the planet. Even in occidental and erudite societies, such as England, the Turing case — precursor of the digital revolution — is emblematic of the prevailing mentality of the half of the XX century. A novel was made out of it and then a movie too, as a moving testament. He can either give up his abnormality or he can be treated with solutions that make him sick. Otherwise he can go to prison. The outcome is suicide.

Nowadays, the politically correct has a diametrically opposed location. The procedure is to legitimize the differences (until what point?). Homophobia is retrograde, reactionary and condemnable.

In the instrument field, the progress of surgery and endocrinology allow to create in the anatomical body what was, in the past, only an unrealizable fantasy. The modification of the border between the technique and the willing body has, therefore, changed the rules of the game. However, the instrument solution does not solve the identity issue that always makes us uneasy. As Daniel Gil has explained, the Kantian obligation of" "Ought implies Can" reverses and nullifies the ethic dimension becoming: "Can implies Ought".

In addition, the digital revolution opens unprecedented paths to promote the erotic meeting. It goes from choosing a partner as if it was the choice of an electrical appliance to avoiding the fear of venereal diseases that were, once, an omnipresent ghost.

Digital communication (with absent bodies) allows to impersonate some different erotic identities, might it be pretending the gender or the age, in order to satisfy the requests of promising partners and with the expectation to get to know and enjoy a wider hue of different experiences. "More is better" is the consumerisms guideline. The commandment of chastity and the phobia of defloration have turned one hundred and eighty degrees.

Paul Virilio has placed in the speed of changes an important key factor for defining the modern age, but it is not only about the immediacy of the information that crosses the planet or the advance of the rapidity of transportation. The change as a rule to subjectivity does not work the same way as a barter between a carriage and a supersonic airplane. The social bonds multiply in an exponential way, but they tend to be more fleeting, ephemeral and superficial.

Data regarding divorce is eloquent in relation to that. The offer and consumption of different and unnecessary objects is unlikely to improve the way we feel towards ourselves... social and political time accelerate and get internalized, the lightness of being is not only directed towards the others but also to ourselves and the contemplative being is a relic of the past. In the internal tryptic of the temporary nature, the present always tries to be red-hot in reduction to a past full of memories and experiences and a future filled with desires and projects. It is the culture of the ephemeral, of the instantaneous. This increase in size of the present, that devours past and future, is isomorphic with the rapture of drug addiction. Now that I have it all...

Without making the definitions sacred, I want to open a new fringe of challenges for our intents of abstinence and neutrality. In other words, if psychoanalysis has always been a window to the sexual intimacy world and, therefore, an axis of comprehension of the global psychic functioning and the prevailing modalities of the social bonds, a current challenge is the understanding of the way in which the cultural changes have an impact on our clinic.

Interpretation and psychic change do not behave anymore as they did before. The Freudian revolution — psychoanalysis — is the product of its creator's genius. Yet, geniuses still pay tribute to the dominant ideas of their era: in Freud's one, the Victorians androcentric moral and the demonization of sex were absolute. Theories change with history.

In the days of the foundation, one century ago, the borders of the public, the private and the intimate sphere were different from now, and much more unclouded. The body's surface covered with a female's swimsuit exemplifies, in an easy way, the change that has occurred between the showable and the not showable. A change from centuries or millenniums of Judeo-Christian history, from the demonization of eroticism (watch the movie "The white ribbon" of Michel Haneke), that has been facilitated by the diffusion of the birth control methods, achieved by the technical progress and the monitoring of the venereal diseases. Orgasmic satisfaction gained ground in opposition to the sacred commandment of the perpetuation of the species and, furthermore, it is legitimizing itself as a premarital custom.

Today the complication is where to position the prohibition. Radical changes that are not necessarily parallel (or in linear causality) with the internal experience. Yet, the desecration of sexuality has a cultural impact of widespread. It is, with no doubt, a progress. However, progress, always carries new problems and challenges.

***

As Freud states in "Group Psychology and the Analysis of the Ego", the rules that regulate the behaviors are not the same when it comes to personal and collective. The collective soul embraces us until we suffocate whereas being one self is a difficult task reserved to few and always insufficient.

Every era or culture produces its prevalent characteristics. At the summit of ours there is contempt for the inheritance and confusion because of the novelties, the consumerism and the ephemeral that replace the cogitative and contemplative subject. Eric Hobsbawm[2] asserts that never before, in the human history, had there been as much lack of awareness and contempt towards traditions as in our days.

Another edge of Freudians perspicacity and teaching is to postulate and display how the sexual behaviors constitute the prototype of our conduct in other fields. The prohibition to the incestuous eroticization is the substructure of other prohibitions and the founder of the culture. The fact that in the act and fantasies, childish sexual experiences combine temptation and guilt, braided in a very peculiar way, is an unavoidable crossroads that reissues itself and formulates again during puberty.

Nowadays the blurred line between the allowed and the transgressive does not only become a manifesto in sexuality's field, but also expands to other areas of the biblical commandments. The relation between the "You shall not murder" and the execution of people at one thousand kilometers through a tele guided missile or the magnitude of corruption in the echelon of politics are symptoms that expand in the planets current issues.

The Bible asserts that God created the world in six days and rested on the seventh, meditating. In this world of vertiginous changes, the analytical experience aims at reestablishing a healthier equilibrium between the transitive (or explosive) times and the reflexive ones of the psychic experience. The tranquility of a Sunday is always necessary.

---

2   Eric Hobsbawm, *Age of Extremes: The Short XX Century, 1944-1991* (Abacus Books, 1994).

THE INTIMACIES OF TRANS-LIVES

Jeanne Wolff Bernstein

Under the sad and dark shadow of Felix de Mendelssohn's death, it is difficult for me not to read the title of the conference *The Dislocated Subject* retrospectively, in a very literal sense, as the subject who is truly located in another place, so out of reach and beyond, that we cannot grasp him anymore. Death does this in a very real way, leaving friends, family and colleagues behind with their share of memories, feelings and thoughts, invoking a melancholic longing for what and who once was, but no longer sadly is.

Felix's sudden and all too premature death made me think that the kinds of subjectivities, I will be addressing, are inherently and intimately very much connected with death, namely the death of the subject and its location as a mere functional other in the Other. In the kinds of practices I will be discussing, subjectivity is ultimately located so far outside of a self, that the self can only survive as an object, an instrument and a mere function both in the eyes of the Other and subsequently of the subject himself. The kinds of trans-bodied intimacies I will be looking at, all started as helpful technological innovations in response to real human suffering, but in the rampant age of globalization — and I would say, dehumanization —, these bio-technological advances have turned into human nightmares and tragedies.

Let us look first at the history of organ transplants:
"Love you to death" has become a literal saying in the 20th and 21th century. A great deal of love can be involved when one person decides to give his/her healthy organ to a fellow human being. Since kidneys are the only human organ of which there are two, and the only ones where one can survive with a single one, most live organ transplants pertain to kidneys. Many brothers and sisters, parents and children are tied by this additional bond when they give their ailing sibling or child one of their own healthy kidneys to enable the survival of their kin. Intrinsically linked by a similar

genetic make-up, they constitute the best and most appropriate "donors" for their relatives. However, complex family dynamics can evolve as one sibling may only begrudgingly and forcibly donate their kidney, while others experience this donation as an act of love and celebrate the date of donation as their second mutually-held birthday. As one donor described these birthdays to me: "My brother has now a wonderful life with his family and my kidney" (A. Sampson, 2016). The lives of the donor and recipient tend to have different destinations, with the recipient typically improving right away, while the donor generally undergoes a more painful and lengthy recuperation due to the removal of a perfectly healthy organ. A dearth of literature exists about the experience of organ transplants in the field of psychoanalysis, but what does exist, primarily focuses on the emotional disturbances accompanying the transplant operations. It is by now, for instance, a well-established fact that many heart-transplant patients experience short-term psychotic episodes after they have received the heart of another human being. For most transplant patients, it takes a while until they adapt to their internal foreign organs and accept them as their own. As Castelnuovo-Tedesco (1973) wrote:

> During regressed mental states, guilt about having 'stolen' the organ may occur together with the feeling that his essential characteristics have been altered as a result of possessing, inside, a part from another human being. Thus some patients are euphoric and feel they have gained special strength as a result of this acquisition, while others, in a more regressed state, feel persecuted by the transplanted organ which they regard as a malignant foreign body. (p. 362)

We are also familiar with the common myth that people receiving a donated organ often adopt, through this transplantation, characteristics of the person from whom they received the organ. In a radio interview, a wife, who had donated one of her kidneys to her ailing husband, spoke of the uncanny fact that her husband had "transitioned" more into his wife, becoming more domestic and homebound, discovering an all too new desire to bake cakes and performing house duties, something he was rather disinclined to do before the spousal transplant operation.

We also know that the acquisition of a foreign organ into one's own body is accompanied by a gradual language development, where the recipient of the organ gradually — at first reluctantly — incorporates the organ into his or her own language. Once the initial euphoria of surviving the transplant operation has passed and the recipient is assured of an extension of his/her life, the recipient tends to become more differentiated, more aware of his/her dependence upon the Other. In a more recent study of a kidney-transplant couple (2008), where a husband had received a kidney from his wife, researchers set out to study the progressive changes within the mind of the recipient through tracking the thoughts, he had written down in his diary:

> On a day like this, I think about the question, "What would have happened if I didn't get a new kidney? It would have certainly been worse, and with no perspective of getting better, it really puts a lot of stress on the family. That's why I am so thankful for my wife, and I know how to treat this gift. Every day I am careful that the amount I drink is enough and that I don't stress and damage it. (*The kidney*, Decker, 2008, p. 245)

The initial reference to "it" and the subsequent correction to "kidney" and later on to the "wife's kidney" at the very end, reveals the recipient's initial reluctance and denial that this organ that has expanded his life and had come from another human being. By calling the kidney "it," the recipient is compelled to deny the humanness of the transaction and the immense dependency and gratitude he may have had experienced towards his wife for giving up her kidney to him.

Specialists in the transplant field have often remarked that recipients' "compliance" rate greatly depends upon their ability to receive and surrender to an Other. Those who can, tend to be far more compliant with the subsequent treatments (medications, etc) while those who are more narcissistically structured and wounded in their sense of omnipotence, cannot tolerate this dependence, and subsequently treat their new organ with as little care and consideration as they had treated their own before. According to Decker, Lehmann, etc.:

> The donor organ offers protection and serves as an idealized self-object, but also takes on very threatening, destructive traits. The donor organ moves as a transitional object in an area between one's own and something foreign. As a result, the potential of inner psychological conflicts to become a symbol is destroyed. The actually introduced object is burdened with archaic feelings of guilt in a highly ambivalent experience. The wife as a donor is linked in the inner imagination of the recipient to the vision of a damaged deprived mother image, whose revenge for this seizure is to be feared. Ambivalences towards the caring mother object can then lead to a qualitative change in the experience off the donor organ. (2008, p. 250)

In a 2012 article in the "International Journal of Psycho-analysis", Goetzman and Boothe remark that, in an initial phase of psychic processing, the recipient identifies with the unknown, simply fantasized donor, during which the patient experiences the transplanted organ as foreign. The identification with the donor rests on incorporation, i.e., the self-image blends with unconscious fantasies about the donor. In contrast the transplant is simply introjected while it is certainly incorporated into the recipient's psychic world, the transplant remains an independent, demarcated object. In this way, the unconscious identification with the donor (via incorporation) appears to ease the assimilation (via introjection) of the transplanted organ... The representation of the donor at first reflects the self-representation of the recipient, then detaches itself gradually, and eventually moves from the core of the self to the external world. The transplant moves into the opposite direction, from the periphery to the core of the self, and ultimately integrates into the recipient's self-image. (pp. 119–120)

But what happens to the process of identification with the donor on the part of the recipient if the donor gives up his kidney to make simply some money to survive, as was the case with a young Chinese boy, who, in 2012, came home with a new I-Pad that he had bought with the money he had earned from donating one of his kidneys in make-shift hospital? Or what about countries where kidneys and other organs are "harvested" as a means of meeting the growing demand for organ transplants. When organ transplants are taken out of hospital settings and become primarily a money-making business, all bets are off as the organ transplant underground shows that developed in Albania, Serbia and China, to name just a few countries. In these countries, prisoners were killed in order to harvest their organs. The grizzly practice of an Albanian gang executing Serbian prisoners in order to extract their kidneys, converting detention facilities into make-shift hospitals came to light in 2010. Some of the guards, interviewed by the NY Times admitted that a few prisoners had figured out their fate and "pleaded with their captors to be spared the fate of being chopped up into pieces." (2010, p. 3)

It is worth think about the word "organ harvesting" for a moment, or "organ legging" for that matter, to realize the degree to which the body, or its individual parts, have come to exist outside of the law in the human mind and are being traded as pure commodities world-wide. Goggle dictionary defines "organ harvesting" as follows:

Organ harvesting refers to the removal, preservation and use of human organs and tissue from the bodies of the recently deceased to be used in surgical transplants on the living. Though mired in an ethical debate and heavily regulated, organ donation in the United States has largely become an accepted medical practice.

"Harvesting" thus implies that crops and seeds can be garnered in one body, only to bear fruit in another, and it can also be equated with the idea of scrounging for leftover "goodies" in an already dead body, as the Israeli practice of removing corneas, skin grafts and heart valves reveals from one body and implanting them in another one. Here the image of an internal bazaar comes to mind where medical technicians — much like Victor Frankenstein — browse through dead bodies to see what they can remove and quickly put to use. Since a kidney may be bid nowadays for as high as $160.000 on the black-trade organ market, the scrounging for left-over bodily parts, brings in a plentiful harvest. "Harvesting" becomes closely aligned with the word "hoarding", implying greed and ruthlessness where the most desperate and poorest human beings are used-abused and often killed to save and serve the richer and more educated ones. A quick look at some of the countries' laws pertaining to organ trade practices also reveals another unsettling practice with regard to how politically motivated some of these organ transplants have become. In India, for instance, "harvested" kidneys from poor Indian laborers are only to be transplanted into bodies of foreign, non-Indian people. The reason for such a firm native/foreign policy was strictly economical since the native was paid $1000 and the foreigner, was asked to pay $37.500. The native/inlander/foreign dimension becomes even more complex in countries like Iran or Israel. After the 1979 Iranian revolution, Iran had faced a donor crisis since there was no cadaveric donation. People either quickly died or travelled abroad to get a new kidney. The government stepped in, deciding to allow transpants from biologically related — then emotionally related — and finally from "altruistic" donors. Despite such an emotionally constructed donor system, 76% of donations came from the "altruistic" donors and only 12% from the 2 other groups. Why this gap? Iran paid, compensating unrelated donors $1200 in addition to the medical costs involved in the after-care of kidney removal and a year of free health insurance. While this appears to be a very generous organ transplant policy, it also had its nationalistic limits, since Iranians can only donate to fellow Iranians and refugees living within Iran, can only donate to fellow refugees, i.e. an Afghan national can only donate to an Afghan refuge (see Griffin, 2007, for a more detailed discussion).This national protectionism has played no role, interestingly enough, in one of the most divisive conflicts in the world, ie. Israel and Palestine. Although Israel initially called these allegations false and anti-semitic, it did eventually admit in 2009, that pathologists at the Abu Kabir Forensic Institute near Tel Aviv had "harvested" organs from dead Palestinians without acquiring the prior consent of their families and without legislating against the possibility that Palestinian hearts could beat in Israeli bodies (Black, The Guardian, December 20, 2009).

What do these national and individual practices tell us about the location of the subject, subjects who are deeply divided and fragmented, ready to sell their own organs in a progressively deteriorating social and economic structure? And, what does the economic and political trade of these part-objects say about the "organ brokers" — the middlemen — who organize and negotiate these bids?

It is true that bodies have always been for sale, for instance, in the slave trades or in prostitution or in human trafficking, and bodies have always been used as weapons and instruments for making political or religious statements as we can see in the suicide bombers or in the freedom fighters who set their own bodies on fire to protest their countries' political demise and religious persecution (See Tunisia). I want to argue that there is a difference between using one's own body, destroying it or selling it, or trading it as a simple piece of flesh that can bargained for all over the world because this practice no longer sees the human body as a whole, but instead privileges "the body in pieces", valuing those pieces over the whole body. When economic conditions are such that the individual can no longer sustain himself, a regression takes place to a primordial level of experience of being a body in pieces, where pieces of a body are put on the black market to maintain a highly impoverished sense of going-on-being. What I am suggesting is that there is a crisis of the imaginary where the poorest people in the world are propelled to live on the edge of the Real where they are confronted daily with the fright of survival. The register of the imaginary no longer holds them together and their decision to allow themselves to be cut up and then to be stitched together is a move back towards the Real where no illusions and no laws protect the human subject from the cruelties of the world. Francisco Gonzales, in response to an earlier version of this paper (JW Bernstein, 2013), characterized the practice of "organ harvesting" as "a slasher-film version of Foucault's concept of biopower, which is driven by ideologies of power and national proliferating technqiues for the subjugation of bodies and the control of populations. Ironically, he writes, this political technology is rooted in nineteenth century notions of public health: census taking, regimes of hygenie, birth controls, the regulation of sexuality through so-called sex education, mental health sanitation." (2013, p. 7)

The practice of surrogacy comes closest to the practice of organ donation, since only one part of the body is used to enable, and in this case, create, not prolong, the life of another human being. Surrogacy has also a long and complex history and is a practice that is allowed in some countries and others, like Germany and Austria, not at all. Like organ transplants, surrogacy is also divided into separate categories, gestational surrogacy (known as host and full surrogacy) and partial, genetic or straight surrogacy. In gestational surrogacy, the result form the transfer of an embryo created by in vitro fertilization (IVF), results in a manner so that the child is genetically unrelated to the surrogate. Gestational surrogates are also referred to as gestational carriers. In traditional surrogacy, the surrogate is impregnated naturally or artificially, but the resulting child is genetically related to the surrogate. If the surrogate receives money for the surrogacy, the arrangement is considered a commercial surrogacy, if she receives no compensation, it is referred to — as in organ transplants — as an altruistic practice. In a similar fashion to organ transplant practices, the technique of commercial surrogacies has gained the upper hand and in conjunction with the sale of "fresh, young" eggs that are harvested and frozen and sperm that can preserved and frozen, wombs are also put up for sale with babies gestating in maternal wombs with whom they have no genetic or in many cases, no emotional connection. India, for instance, has remained a main destination for surrogacy, because of the relatively low costs. Entire villages have been created in India where young women come together for the period of their pregnancies, under the care of maternity clinics. They live with another until they bear the child for their destined foreign couple. After having been paid a substantial sum for their surrogacy, they leave this "birthing" community for their home until they are called back again for another nine months of a surrogacy pregnancy. One might say that pregnancy is nowadays outsourced to poor countries like India for wealthy, infertile couples from Western countries.

Wombs have also been used — much like the transplanted organs — for political purposes, in other words, for settling scores among enemies. The most recent use of a politically motivated pregnancy was made public when it became known that a number of Palestinian women had successfully smuggled out the sperms of their husbands serving life sentences in an Israeli prison. Defying the strict Israeli security measures, these women were pleased to bear young new "freedom fighters" in Ramalla. In contrast to the Palestinian women who elected to be impregnated by their jailed husbands, the young women, kidnapped by Boko Haram, were forcibly impregnated with the sperm of the imprisoners in order to proliferate their home countries with little warriors produced by soldiers faithful to Boko Haram. "They turned me into a sex machine" reported one woman, repeatedly raped by adherents to Boko Harem (NY Times, May, 2015). One interesting exception exists though among ISIS fighters in Iraq who rape the women they imprison and buy, yet "enforce birth control on their sex slaves" as the NY Times reports (NY Times, March 21, 2016).

According to an obscure ruling in Islamic law, a man must ensure that the woman he enslaves is free of a child before having intercourse with her. Islamic State leaders have made sexual slavery as they believe it was practiced during the Prophet Muhammad's time, integral to the groups' operations, preying on the women and girls the group captured from the Yazidid religious minority. To keep the sex trade running, the fighters have pushed for birth control" (NY Times, March 21, 2016). For the young women under this ISIS control, pregnancy thus becomes an act of liberation, because no ISIS soldier will touch her if she is pregnant.

We can see throughout all these examples I have presented that the new technological means with which an organ failure could be repaired or an infertility could be cured, constituted procedures which were designed to address human suffering and loss. Through organ transplants millions of lives are nowadays saved who would have simply died some 50 years ago. What had once perhaps been a mere phantasy, cutting out the organ out of one body and placing it into another one to save or prolong that body's life, has become a reality, an affordable and even profitable one. I would like to argue that the modern practice of organ transplants have concretized Karl Abraham's and Freud's concept of incorporation, which Laplanche defines as follows:

> Process whereby the subject, more or less on the level of phantasy, has an object penetrate his body and keeps it inside his body. Incorporation constitutes an instinctual aim and a mode of relationship which are characteristic of the oral stage, although it has a special relationship with the mouth and with the ingestion of food, it may also be lived out in relation with other erotogenic zones and other functions. Incorporation provide the corporal mode for introjection and identification... During the oral stage... the act of obtaining erotic mastery over an object coincides with that object's destruction. (211–212)

After Freud's *Mourning and Melancholia* (1915/1917), Abraham elaborated upon the cannibalistic and possessive tendencies of both the oral and anal drive, suggesting that "Psychoanalytic experience has shown beyond a doubt that in the middle stage of his libidinal development, the individual regards the person who is the object of his desire as something over which he exercises ownership, and that he consequently treats that person in the same way as he does his earliest piece of private property, i.e. the contents of his body, his faeces. Whereas on the genital level, love means the transference of his positive feeling on to the object and involves a psych-sexual adaptation to that object, on the level below it means that he treats his object as though it belonged to him." (1924, 426)

In a much later paper, Maria Torok and Nicolas Abraham separate out more clearly the narcissistic aspects of the process of introjection versus the process of internalization by explaining that incorporation is the result of a failed mourning process, where no gradual mourning has taken place, but where the process is fast, unmediated, magical and sometimes hallucinatory. They write (1972/1994): "The phantasy of incorporation betrays a hole in the soul, a lack at precisely the location, where an introjection should have taken place." (p. 131)

Introjection takes place where internalization has failed. We are living in a world where mourning is increasingly and rapidly becoming a process of the past since technology has always aimed at stuffing and speeding up the holes left behind by human misery and loss. Confronted with a potentially fatal disease or years at a dialysis machine, or faced with the prospect of a childless relationship, we have now mastered the techniques of filling up these losses and making them available to millions of people. However, once these losses are turned into economic profits, once the law has stepped aside and made room for the global market to become the world-wide regulator, the anal, greedy and ruthless aspects of this loving gesture of "gifting" shows its ugly, sadistic and profiteering underside. Love and hate, as Freud so often noted, have to wrestle with one another, and in this age of perversion where human beings are functioning more and more like machines and where machines become more human, we need to become increasingly watchful of the degradation and inhumanity we are facing in the all too human desire to create and expand lives beyond the expectable barriers. Ever since Prometheus, whose name means *Foreknowledge,* was punished by Zeus for his thrust to provide fire as a source of light and warmth for human mortals, fellow scientists have always dared to trespass the given laws to provide new comforts to the world. A promethean push towards the future cannot be stopped, and once the fire is stolen, it cannot be returned, no matter what the human consequences may be. However, psychoanalysis cannot afford to be a silent bystander to this rapidly shifting world of transplanted organs, shifting wombs and the dispension of fertile eggs and sperms. Psychoanalysis has to stay tuned to these technological changes and re-situate the subjects into newly-created constellations, reminding the human subjects time and again that the new technological devices of and for the bodies, forebode both a sense of hope and exhilaration but also bear a terrifying potential for tragedy. And yet, as Maureen Murphy in her paper *Assisted Reproduction and the Fate of Desire* (2010) writes, "We (psychoanalysts), are challenged to stay in the game, to abandon the body to the scientists would be to irrevocably splinter our work. It is our job to preserve the libidinization of the body in the midst of medical advance." (p. 8)

References

Abraham, K., 'A Short Study of the Development of Libido Viewed in the Light of Mental Disorders', in *Selected Papers of Karl Abraham* (The International Psycho-Analytical Library, 1924), pp. 418–501.

Abraham, N. and Torok, M., 'Mourning and Melancholia: Introjection versus Incorporation', in *The Shell and the Kernel* (Chicago: The University of Chicago Press, 1972–1994), pp. 125–138.

Author Unknown, 'Five Face Charges in China over Sale of Youth's Kidney', New York Times, April 2007 (2012).

Black, I., The Guardian, 20 December 2009, p. 13.

Castelnuovo-Tedesco, P., 'Organ Transplant, Body Image, Psychosis', The Psychoanalytic Quarterly, 42 (1973), 349–363.

Carvajal, D. and Simons, M., 'Report Names Kosovo Leader as Crime Boss', New York Times, 15 December 2010.

Decker, O., Lehmann, A., Fangman, J., Brosig, B., and Winter, M., 'Phases of organ integration and conflict in a transplant recipient: A longitudinal study using a diary', The American Journal of Psychoanalysis, 68 (2008), 237–256.

Freud, S., 'Mourning and Melancholia', in *The Standard Edition of the Complete Psychological Works of Sigmund Freud*, Vol. 14 (London: The Hogarth Press, XXI, 1915 [1917]), pp. 237–260.

Goetzman, L., Boothe, B., Boehler, A., and Neukom, M., 'Fantasized Recipient-Donor Relationships following Lung Transplantations: A Qualitative Case Analysis Based on Patient Narratives', International Journal of Psycho-Analysis, 93, 117–137.

Gonzalez, F., 'Making Bodies: A Discussion of Papers by Maureen Murphy and Jeanne Wolff Bernstein', Fort/Da, 19 (2013), 50–57.

Griffin, A., The British Medical Journal, 334 (2007), #7592, 502–507.

Lacan, J., 'The Mirror Stage as Formative of the I Function as Revealed in Psychoanalytic Experience', in *Ecrits*, trans. by Bruce Fink (New York: W. W. Norton & Co, 2002 [1949]).

Laplanche, J. and Pontalis, J.B., *The Language of Psychoanalysis*, trans. by Donahl Nicholson-Smith (London: Karnac Books, 1973).

Murphy, M., 'Assisted Reproduction and Fate of Desire', unpublished paper, 2010, pp. 1–10.

Nossiter, A., 'Boko Haram Militants Raped Hundred of Female Captives in Nigeria', New York Times, 18 May 2015.

Rukmini, C., 'The Culture of Rape Within ISIS, and the Questions That Arise', New York Times, March 21 (2016).

Wolff Bernstein, J., Organ-Legging, the Mother of all Body Transplantations, Fort/Da, Vol. 19 (2013), pp. 39–49.

ZOMBIE HYPERCALYPS(IS)

Paolo Fabbri

The monster is a semiotic reminder, a social semiophor, a grotesque ornament of our mediascape. Its imaginary significance (supernatural), shifts in response to the new interdefinitions that involve it: with respect to the new status of animals and robots, the discipline of automation.

The paleo-monster that lurked and ambushed us in our collective imaginary was the effect of an ambivalent sentiment of attraction/repulsion, pity, and fascination with the animal world. With those nearer to us, subject to domestication (pets, livestock) and those more distant (game animals and wild beasts). But once biotechnology has signaled the end of domestication — with stables and barns — "beasts" must cease to be Cartesian protein-based machines. And they will become, with us, the actants of a new contract of co-domestication, foretold by Aesop, Phaedrus, and Lafontaine. It has even been suggested (and so far rejected) that we extend the Declaration on the Rights of Man to include the great apes!

The monster becomes the attractor and repulsor of a new hybridization of man and machine; the monstrous machine is not the robot, but the Cyborg, which has long been hypothesized, dreamed of, and debated in terms of the "post-human," or the "Terminator." And the 'sex appeal of the inorganic,' (Perniola) with the commingling of automatisms of every grade and order, mechanical and digital; a hybrid cross between human and inhuman; an understandable mutation in the digital age of cerebral machines pulsing with 'angels,' that is, with messengers both analog and digital, frozen and disembodied (Savinio).

There is, in any case, an (ugly) semiophor that shows that the West can still produce fables and that "Myths can continue to flow" (Wittgenstein). A new collective actant, the current apex of monstrosity, which does not meld nature and culture, the animate and the inanimate, but situates itself between life and death: the zombie. The Undead, an exo-darwinian figure evolved from the Caribbean *ghol* of A&I, and coming to occupy, brainless as it is, the neural laboratories and manuals of analytic philosophy (by the name of Zimbo). "This disconcerting fantasy helps make the problem of phenomenal consciousness vivid (sic!) especially as a problem for physicalism," says the *Stanford Encyclopedia of Philosophy* in the lengthy entry dedicated to it.

The Undead, testaments to a macabre, suburban decadence, have become the icons of globalization. The sinister site of their abandoned burial-grounds — Zombistan — has infiltrated the collective imaginary to the point of producing carnivalesque city parades of neogothic and grotesque masks. A Bakhtinian Halloween in which the gardens return to their origin, the cemetery, just as the contemporary cities to the Necropolis. Swarms of young activists, between protest and parody, participate *perinde ac cadaver* in festive and civic-minded marches of half-rotten Undead. The dead do not laugh, but the Undead do bite. "One laughs instead of devouring" (Canetti); the infected bite of the zombie is replaced with the laugh of the costumed simulators. These are the "Zombie walks," semi-spontaneous flash mobs, alternative performances with respect to the processional model of political marches.

The zombie, an imperfect corpse, is resituated in a new cladistics of the horror genre, in a teratological taxonomy that has been redistributed. The Undead now staggers definitively into the contemporary mediasphere; it is a new syllable of semantic content in the word "Horror. Its foul genre occupies a place of prominence in the imaginary biodiversity of de-massified culture. Its survival strategy obligates it to adapt to the environment and strive to endure. It has already faced off against all the superheroes, from Spiderman to the Hulk, from Giant-man to Wolverine. It has been placed in relation and in tension with all the figures of horror: Devils and robots, cyborgs and aliens, replicants and clones, ghosts and mummies, werewolves and body snatchers, extraterrestrials and vampires, with which it shares some similar differences. "The zombie, solidly intra-terrestrial with its corrupt physicality, is the opposite of the ectoplasmic angels and ghosts and of the mechanical perfection of the robot... Among the dead returning from their conservation society, the zombie reawakens like the mummy or the skeleton, from which it stands apart due to its state of decomposition. The Skeleton is dry and articulated like the robot, while the undead provokes disgust for the advanced rottenness that deforms and discolors it; the Mummy, better preserved, for good reason, sits between the skeleton and the zombie that shares, along with the Golem, its uncertain gait. But it is in the vampire that the Undead finds its more toothy rival in sepulchral semantics, due to their shared cannibal instincts. A "mytheme"(Lévi-Strauss) with the same "emergent" properties, but differing in lifestyle and nourishment:

the Vampire is (still, but not for much longer) the elegant inhabitant of abodes and sepulchers, while the zombies frequent common graves and middle-class supermarkets, amusement parks, prison islands, and even the set of Big Brother; the seductive, however degraded, Vampire sucks blood from the erogenous zones, while the zombies, just barely escaping the incinerator, rise all rumpled from their caskets and devour strips of human flesh on the spot, raw and unseasoned." We have already said so elsewhere (Fabbri), but one trait still demands our attention. Zombie is the collective name for rebels against the cadaveric tautologies of ontology: "the dead lie and the living have peace." The Undead, however, do not join the choir invisible of the dead — the "mighty masses of the Afterlife" (Canetti) — with which they still share some salient traits: openness, growth, rhythmic slowness, equality, concentration, etc. Zombies are a rhizome in motion, a wolfpack of Deleuzian memory, a collective permanently straining towards a single end: the hunt for man. A prey that, from the spiteful perspective of the dead, does not deserve to survive. The pack — which in Italian, *muta,* is, etymologically, movement, revolt, and hunting party — is turned obsessively to the communion of an unspoken collective meal. "They all grab, bite, chew, swallow the same thing" (Canetti), that is human beings, reduced to a disintegrated mass. Leaving out the theme of altruism, C. Lévi-Strauss, reasoning on cannibalism, saw the social life as "the lower limit of predation" and held that "All told, the simplest means of identifying the other with one's self is still to eat it." Collective cohabitation would be the effect of the deliberate suspension of the primary, devouring difference between prey and predator, and the Zombie is one regressive suspension of this stabilization.

Zombies horrify us because they are not. They, the radically Other; they are both Us and You, with a humanity that revolts us due to the atrocious suspicion that we are a part of it. But furthermore, they frighten us as protagonists of the "Hypercalypse" of postmodern pandemics, the mass extinctions that occupy the whole planet as their theater of operations. In fiction, the Undead represent the epidemic noise that infests humanity's state of health, the infective and viral manifestation of death in its return to life. Their planetary conquest anticipates and perhaps foretells a hecatombic, obsidional world. The Living who survive, besieged by hunters in sectarian islands, must re-kill the rebellious, risen Zombies, while they infect the living and revive them as Undead. Life resists death and the Undead assails life. Like a kamikaze, it advances toward its living adversary without fear of re-dying. The comprehensive result is the end of all forms of burial and a non-humanity, uncivil — as Vico would say — because unburied. Consecrated, therefore, to the ghosts that devour their own flesh: necrophobia and necrophilia. In the techno-scientific simulation there already exists a diagnostic model of these paradoxical parasites, with calculated prognoses. To eradicate the infection requires quantifiable reductions in the number of Zombies: with swift and violent strikes, one might avoid the collapse of humanity, overcome by the new, extinct barbarians. It is, indeed, the Hypercalypse.

It is difficult, if not acrobatic, to correlate the brainless swarms of the monstrous imaginary with the whole of the socio-cultural collective, with the social history of technology and the idea of the human, but it is in the heart of our mythologies that the anti-behavior of the living provokes the contact with the dead. How to avoid, then, turnkey sociological solutions: the zombie as a social hieroglyph, "a symptom of cultural dissatisfaction and economic crisis" and other solecisms: desacralization and modernization, and so on? And yet, notwithstanding everything, what we are expecting etymologically from the Hypercalypse are revelations that respond to the most cogent questions about individual necrosis and collective narcosis. On the current status of the person, identity and belonging, rendered fluid by medicine: are patients in a deep coma — PVS, persistent vegetative state — still alive (almost-subjects) or undead (almost-objects)? Still. The biblical exigency that the dead bury the dead was an extraditionary precaution to impede the permanence of the deceased as unwieldy Ancestors. Ritually weeping to liberate, or at least clarify the future. Now the Undead, Lazaruses reawakened from unknown transcendences, add an inescapable "historical" interrogative to the present of the living: "How do we live with the experiences of the past? Without the pressure of planning for the future?!" In terms of contemporary presentism, are the living and the Undead not, perhaps, equivalent?

In the absence of answers, the decomposing, cannibal images of the Zombie will continue to trouble our dreams.

References

Baudrillard, J., *L'Echange symbolique et la mort* (Paris: Gallimard, 1976).
Brooks, M., *The Zombies Survival Guide*, (Random House, 2003).
Canetti, E., *Masse und Macht*, 1960.
Christie, D., Lauro, S. (eds.), *Better Off Dead: The Evolution of the Zombie as PostHuman* (New York: Fordham University Press, 2011).
Coulombe, M., *Petite philosophie du zombie* (Paris: PUF, 2012).

Eco, U., 'I nostri mostri quotidiani', in *Apocalittici e Integrati* (Milan: Bompiani, 1964).

Fabbri, P., 'Yes, we Zombies can', AutAut, Il saggiatore (Milan, 2013).

Guy, H., Jeanjean, A., Richier, A., 'Le cadavre en procès: une introduction', Techniques & Culture, 60 (2013).

(Kirk, R.), 'Zombie', in *Stanford Enciclopedia of Philosophy* (Stanford: Stanford Univ. Press, 2013).

Lévi-Strauss, C., *Nous sommes tous des cannibales* (Paris: Seuil, 2013).

Métreaux, A., *Le voudou haitien* (Paris: Gallimard, 1958).

Moreman, Ch.M., Rushton, C.J. (eds.), *Zombies Are Us: Essays on the Humanity of the Walking Dead* (McFarland, 2011).

'Mutants', Critique, n. 709-10, juin-juillet 2006.

Perniola, M., *Il sexappeal dell'inorganico* (Turin: Einaudi, 2004).

Yuen, W., *The Walking Dead and Philosophy: Zombie Apocalypse Now* (Open Court, 2012).

INTO THE DARKNESS.
A TRIP THROUGH VIRTUAL SPACES[1]

Mariano Horenstein

> Then he moved on, and I behind him followed.
> Dante, *The Divine Comedy*

The Blind Guide

There are some terrains that should not be visited without a guide. For many psychoanalysts, Freud takes on the role of a guide. Today I want to propose a different sort of guide, one that leads me through a terrain that at moments seems like Hell, a Hell in permanent mutation, that of virtual spaces. For someone like me, a member of *Generation X* who functions in a digital world without having been born in a digital era, a guide could be a youth trained to use the latest technology, a millennial. Nowadays, it is not uncommon to see young people teaching adults.

As Virgil led Dante, Borges, the most universal writer of my native land, will lead me through the hells and paradises of our contemporary virtualization. Borges was born in Buenos Aires at the time Freud was writing his books on dream interpretation here...

It seems difficult to believe that a blind 80-year-old poet who wrote by hand or dictation, and who dreamed of a world of bandits and tango singers, Bengal tigers, never-ending mirrors and labyrinths, could possibly know the world we want to explore here.

But then again, if you think about the richness of Argentina and of its people, it is also difficult to believe that we could always be in a state of underdevelopment. Perhaps you think that we somehow manage. After all, a Pope, a Queen and the best soccer player in the world have come out of Argentina; and Borges too; and the greatest density of psychoanalysts per square meter in the world.

The choice of our Virgil is not so unbelievable if we consider two things: One is his blindness. And since psychoanalysis stems from the

---

1   I would like to dedicate this text — the written version of the conference held at Freud Museum in 2016 — to Miguel Leivi, master and friend, who knows — better and before than me — the subject which I have talked about in Vienna.

epistemological shift that replaced the Gaze in curing ailments of the soul for that of Listening, we are on solid ground.

As a guide, Borges is anachronic; as anachronic as Freud or psychoanalysis itself. Far from being a defect announcing its uselessness, anachronism is the very key to psychoanalysis' efficacy.

Borges predicted the future we live now:[2] the virtual spaces. He could do this because he went against the tide, against any contemporary ambition. He saw the future because he didn't care about predicting it; his foreignness — isomorphic to that of the psychoanalyst — was necessary for his finely-tuned ability to listen.

If science hadn't ceased to be a way of telling stories,[3] psychoanalysis probably would have never existed. This scientific discourse wouldn't have excluded the subject or his experience. Here is our science of singularity, weak in pure scientific terms, but unrivaled when considering the human discontent. Psychoanalysis is — as Pierre Legendre said — almost an accident of scientific thought.

Borges wouldn't disapprove of this definition.

An Imaginary Hell

Remember when Virgil led Dante through Hell, that funnel-like space where sinners burned for an eternity. As they descended from one concentric circle to another, the graveness of sins and the lack of space they were condemned to live in, increased. For those interested in the role of space in mental configuration, this fact is critical. As *Geographies of Psychoanalysis* proposes, depriving ourselves of space can be a curse.

By Virgil's hand, Dante witnessed the eternal torments endured by the lustful, the greedy, the avaricious and the prodigal, the angry and the lazy, the heretics, the violent, the frauds and the traitors. Our Hell will be that of the virtual space, technology has superimposed, like a new map on the mind's landscape and the relationships that analysts have explored for the past century.

The first circle of our Hell is the most superficial and an entrance into the rest: the web. It's difficult to imagine our existence without it, although a few decades ago it didn't exist. We are far from understanding

---

2   Perla Sasson-Henry, *Borges 2.0. From text to virtual worlds* (New York: Peter Lang Publishing, 2007).

3   Neil Postman (1992), p. 154, cit. in M. Santos, *A natureza do espacio* (São Paulo: Editora da Universidade de São Paulo, 2006).

the consequences of the appearance and installation of the internet as an omnipresent virtual net. One of its essential characteristics, seemingly opposite to our normal behavior, is its affinity with the surface.

When Baricco talks about the surface and analyzes the phenomenon of contemporary mutations,[4] he describes his barbarians, the millennials, as surface animals. Depth is foreign to this generation, as is psychoanalysis, or the so-called depth psychology. But these mutant youths navigate amazingly on the surface, gaining in velocity what they lose in depth, and the map they build extends like water on a flat surface which offers no resistance. Within this terrain, we should somehow make a space for psychoanalysis and the experience we propose to our patients. However, it is not always that easy.

Borges imagined this web in a way in *The Library of Babel*[5] when he imagined the universe as a complete and infinite library.

There are many circles due to the existence of the web. From a psychoanalyst's point of view, some are more monstrous than others. Perhaps one of the most interesting of the contemporary phenomena is *Wikipedia*, which invites users to interact and participate. Although one could criticize it, this formidable collaborative encyclopedia is essential. Borges also saw it in *Tlön Uqbar Orbius Tertius*, the marvellous story of a collectively-imagined world superimposed on yet another imaginary world.

One key characteristic to understanding the effectiveness of the web is *hypertext*, connected to *link*, and which made possible the development of a tool central to navigating the web, that of the *Google* search engine. Its own name has been converted to a generic one: if Hell is *Dantesque*, the unconscious *Freudian*, "to search the web" is to *google* it.

One century ago, a text configured as hypertext, as they are on the web, would be a nuisance for readers, disturbing the line of argument or story. But thought functions the same way. As analysts, we know how each word is able to function like a switch at a railway junction, leading one to different destinies that later take on a meaning which is always new. The talking in analysis, free association, and its counterpart — free-floating attention — is a method that is perhaps more akin to the structure of thinking.

The analytic method would be hyper-textual, *avant la lettre*.

Borges predicted hypertext in his short-story *The Garden of Forking Paths*.[6]

---

4   Alessandro Baricco, *Los bárbaros. Ensayo sobre la mutación* (Barcelona: Anagrama, 2012).

5   Jorge Luis Borges, 'La biblioteca de Babel' (1941), in *Obras Completas*, Tome I (Buenos Aires: Emecé, 1989).

6   See Jorge Luis Borges, 'El jardín de los senderos que se bifurcan' and also

One might think that there is nothing sinful about these contemporary characteristics of the relationships we have among us, through technology. However, they are the condition, and for this reason I have placed them on the surface of the Hell I am exploring, in which the ego — that precarious yet self-sufficient instance that psychoanalysis has studied so much — expands with the register that is most similar to it, the imaginary. Let's go further down.

I won't stop to question the superficiality with which we use a variety of terms in the most popular social network, *Facebook*. We all know that *friends, share* and *like* have nothing to do with their actual counterparts. What I am interested in is how each person presents himself there, where from the beginning, from his own name, the priviledged dimension of the image is included.

Everyone creates a profile, a public ego, imaginary, fictitious in the worst way, a construction: smiling images of friends, travelling the world, deciding what belongings and references to show. In this circle of hell, millions of FB users transmit versions of themselves in the way they would like to be seen. In no way is there a relationship to how they really see themselves, and here perhaps the neurosis has mutated: to have fewer than 200 friends could be a catastrophe for many...

FB is an exercise in self-fiction and there's nothing wrong with that. However, it is the opposite of what we try to achieve in analysis: to distance ourselves from the image that represents us, one that is more often than not, coerced by some Ideal, and the mistrust generated from that pretended self-sufficiency one offers up to others.

As we descend further into Hell, the devotion to images is even more extensive. So much so, that there seems to be little space, not even virtual, available to accommodate such a legion of sinners.

Although FB provides space for more and more images, this is potentiated even more so in *Youtube*. This network outdoes FB with the slogan: *Broadcast yourself.*

A curious phenomenon occurs there: more and more young people listen to music through this network where the *visual* is predominant, and not because there aren't other networks, such as *Spotify*. You cannot dispense with what is seen even when listening. What you hear, without images that accompany it, seems to suffer from some disability.

'Examen de la obra de Herbert Quain', both in 'Ficciones' (1944), in *Obras Completas*, Tome I (Buenos Aires: Emecé, 1989) Cf. Perla Sassón-Henry, *Borges 2.0. From Text to Virtual Worlds* (New York: Peter Lang, 2007).

Another circle of hell through which Borges guides us, is that of the *Instagram* users. From its beginning, images have taken the leading role. Anyone who has contact with young people knows the place *Instagram* occupies in their exchanges. We are always late: we learned to use email when it was already outdated for them. Later, we get up the nerve to create a profile on FB only to realize that it had already been displaced by other networks. We had familiarized ourselves with SMS, simple text messages, when WhatsApp appeared, announcing that we still belong to the universe of digital illiterates; we are always lagging behind the next generation. There is a certain delay — the delay of words in relation to images — which seems inseparable from the figure of the psychoanalyst.

In some way, psychoanalysts are powerless against a culture that is transmitted largely through images. For us, the images do not have the same status and we tend to think that a culture that prefers the image devalues the precious power of words.

The discipline of Looking isn't foreign to the psychoanalyst, but the discovery of the unconscious as well as the invention of the analytical atmosphere, happened *a posteriori* and overthrew the culture of the image. Hysteria was treated according to the medical perspective, as shown in the Charcotean theatre of La Salpètriere. It wouldn't be strange to imagine all that iconography by the photographer of hysteria, as Charcot liked to identify himself- populating *Instagram* accounts, if they had existed...

Without leaving the circle of *Instagramers*, we come to another even deeper circle, the *Snapchat* users. Its fundamental characteristic is its instantaneity. Here, photos are exchanged: the pictures are only displayed on the screen of the receiver fleetingly, for seconds.

Borges also imagined this when he invented the fictitious book of sand, of infinite pages, with arbitrary numbering and permanent change, like sand, and neither has a beginning nor an end. Every teenager who sends a photo to his friends repeats the gesture of the story character who offers the book to the narrator, proposing that he look at the illustration of a small anchor.

Look well — he says. It shall not be seen again.

After which the narrator, upon closing the book, immediately opens it again, to search in vain for the image that had disappeared from its pages.[7]

---

7   Jorge Luis Borges, 'El libro de arena' (1975), *Obras Completas*, Tome III (Buenos Aires: Emecé, 1989).

I wonder if room is made for listening in this hellish world of images; how can we dig a hole in images that appear always complete, full, absolute. Listening requires time while the image offers instantaneity. In this part of Hell no one waits, a satisfactory image never arrives, a bulimia of images calls for more and more, you are never satisfied.

Borges always toyed with the idea of having a double, as when he writes:

> Besides, I am destined to perish, definitively, and only some instant of my-self can survive in the other. Little by little, I am giving over everything to him, though I am quite aware of his perverse custom of falsifying and magnifying things.[8]

Something like this happens in the deepest circle of Hell, almost a logical consequence of the above.

Never before have we seen such powerful interfaces and such real simulations, where a large mass of people decide that a second life on the web is more interesting than the first one. That's what many of those decide when they subscribe to a virtual world called *Second Life*, which has more inhabitants — called residents — than my own country.

A *Second Life* user builds his avatar with the illusion of self-procreation, founds his business, buys properties, chooses a sexual partner, visits the psychoanalyst... Reality becomes the place of dreams and it is in the virtual universe where relationships, desires and rivalries unfold; where you have a "real" virtual life. If we could consider real, the life of the protagonist of *The Truman Show* or the millions of human creatures cultivated by machines such as Neo before being awakened by Morpheus in *The Matrix*.

Here we find that it is unnecessary to undo the distortions that the dreamwork imposes, since phantasies appear all around. *Second Life* is about an ideal life. The avatars are usually young and beautiful, like the substitutes in the film *Surrogates* or the beauty of the operating system embodied by Scarlett Johansson's voice in *Her*.

What the users of *Second Life* teach us does not have to do with the delicate Freudian counterpoint between the historical reality and the material one, or the way each one captures reality through his phantasy. It is not even a self-fiction about a narcissistic ego shaping its experiences with a false autonomy. Nor is it one of those subtle games in which Borges imagines another Borges, and through which he could grasp the identifying complexities of subjectivity. It is something else: someone drops out of the

---

8   Jorge Luis Borges, 'Borges y yo' (1960), in 'El Hacedor', in *Obras Completas*, Tome I (Buenos Aires: Emecé, 1989).

world order, symbolic and also real, to carry out an imagined life as if one were a video game's character.

Here, the Freudian formula that proposed to change neurotic misery into ordinary misfortune — the analytic offer and bet — seems powerless against those who choose to become citizens of an imaginary country rather than being responsible citizens of their own desires, in an unfortunate — though real — First Life.

Nobody seems to wake up from this dream superimposed on the reality that Borges, once again, glimpsed at in *The Circular Ruins*. The last sentences of his story could well be the story of an analytic session where a patient finally becomes aware of his subjection by the Other:

> With relief, with humiliation, with terror, he understood that he also was an illusion, that someone else was dreaming him.[9]

Having chosen Borges to explore this Hell does not mean that everything is prefigured and there is nothing new under the sun. But Borges, who was not enthusiastic of psychoanalysis, appears here as a *proto-analyst*.

Through anachronism and blindness, Borges saw beyond and could guess much of what is happening today.

Anachronism, a time-shifter, provides the necessary distance in order to see the present; it is like a healthy estrangement that allows us to think about ourselves.

Blindness is another matter; it's not a bad idea to imagine the psychoanalyst as a myopic animal.

Listening and Gazing

Imagine a storm. Lightning lights up the night, and then a few seconds later, you hear thunder. That scene, common to everyone, reveals how two manifestations emerge from a single event, one visual, the other auditory. The visual is instantaneous, multiple, protean. The auditory, however, is more difficult to capture, is delayed in perception and dissipates to the point of inaudibility. The speed of light — 900,000 times greater than the speed of sound — gives priority to the visual. We see more easily than we hear.

---

9   *Las ruinas circulares* (1944), en Jorge Luis Borges, *Obras Completas*, Tome I (Buenos Aires: Emecé, 1989).

Time is a key factor here. While the visual experience is instantaneous, the auditory experience requires a temporal unfolding to be appreciated. So, it is easier to see than to hear. For this reason psychoanalysis requires a considerable amount of time compared to the immediacy that prevails in hell's circles. Furthermore, listening captures something that is lost in seeing.

In cinema, that which is seen predominates over that which is heard, but the sound recording and what happens offscreen is central. The filmmaker Bresson knew well when he said that *the eye is superficial; the ear is deep and inventive. Whereas the eye goes outward, the ear goes inward.*[10] Audition is also the more predominant sense in poetry. As D.H. Lawrence said: *ears go deeper than eyes can see.*

The pre-Socratic philosophers intuited this when they gave their lectures behind heavy curtains. The words took on a different value when their bodies were invisible to their students, and the spoken words were extracted from the immediate visual surroundings. The *acousmatic* experience[11] is recovered in the analytic atmosphere where the analyst is located outside of the patient's visual field to privilege the register of the voice.

Foucault studied how the medical model is set within the epistemological space of the Gaze,[12] as it is shown in the charcotean theatre of hysteria or in the simple etimology of the auscultation instrument. There the clinician — as part of his research — hears bodily sounds through a simple apparatus, the *stethoscope*. This word comes from *stetos*, thorax, and *scopia*, to look. Although he appears to be listening, the clinician is looking.

The psychoanalyst, on the other hand, blinds himself voluntarily. And like every blind person, he develops other senses vicariously, mostly hearing. Though he seems to be looking, the psychoanalyst is listening.[13]

Psychoanalysis is a place where one speaks and where one is heard. If you think about it, it isn't common to find places where one talks, and fewer still are the places where one is heard.

The Anachronic Sound of Vinyl

If Hell is the place where images spread like metastasis…is Paradise a place where you listen?

---

10   Robert Bresson, *Notas sobre el cinematógrafo* (Madrid: Ardora, 1997).

11   José Halac, *El oído: cantos y encantos en un sentido revolucionario*, Calibán-Revista Latinoamericana de Psicoanálisis, 13, 2 (2015), FEPAL, Montevideo.

12   Michel Foucault, *El nacimiento de la clínica* (México: Siglo XXI, 1966).

13   B. Miguel Leivi, *El síntoma en la clínica psicoanalítica*, http://www.apdeba.org/wp-content/uploads/022001leivi.pdf, accessed in September 2016.

We could think of psychoanalysis' place in the virtual hyper-technological world that we talk about, using a figure that many of you surely recognize, and it has to do with sound support. Let's look at another trait of Borges that makes him the perfect guide.

Psychoanalysis unfolds within the dimension of sound, the material we use in our practice are both the heard and spoken words. Although other senses are present, they work together to give coherency within the field of Listening. It is here where psychoanalysis clearly sets itself apart from the Medical Gaze.

Sound recordings have changed dramatically over time, like so many other things in our lives. Technological evolution is dizzying and music lovers who a few decades ago listened to vinyl records on a phonograph or record player already have problems getting hold of these traditional formats today.

We are currently witnessing a strange phenomenon: the revival of old vinyl records. Not only do we see a return to the production of vinyl records but we also see new designs that are fragile, impractical in size, possessing a limited capacity, and which have wonderful cover designs. Vinyl records have considerable value, and they are a luxury compared to the almost zero cost of some bits of information placed in an iPod.

It is worth asking why and who would pay for that anachronically, impractical and expensive way to store and listen to music. Anyone who has heard a vinyl record knows why. The anachronism of listening to music this way allows us to recover a certain mystery that the digital world annihilates. The same happens when we examine digital and analogue photography. We find that digital recordings flatten the sound; by compressing it, nuances are lost and may be heard again only with vinyl records. The crackling noise of the record needle can be annoying for many but for others, it adds a wonderful aura. The crackling noise recovers what the image hides so that the music may be heard another way.

The same applies to analysis. So-called progress has developed molecules able to modify or suppress anxiety, improve mood, annihilate hallucinations, silence delusions, without a doubt. Progress has also been reported — perhaps less clearly — in the field of non-psychoanalytic psychotherapies. It would be foolish to oppose these therapies, just as it would be foolish to refuse to listen to music on the cell phone or watch movies on Netflix.

But our task, though difficult to accept, goes against the grain. It is anachronistic by structure, if we understand anachronism the way Agamben did,[14] and by doing so shine light on the present. It is an analogue islet — a

---

14   Giorgio Agamben, *¿Qué es lo contemporáneo?*, 2008 (http://19bienal.fundacion paiz.org.gt/wp-content/uploads/2014/02/agamben-que-es-lo-contemporaneo.pdf).

divan is an analogue artifact in a virtual world. Without electrical power, we can't turn on the computer or activate any social network. However, you can still continue talking and listening.

As it is necessary to understand how a person is virtualized, is dislocated and made more complex, it is also necessary to accept that our practice goes against the tide, even though we use *Skype*, have a profile on *Facebook*, or *google* terms or authors that interest us. Although we see conferences on *Youtube* and write texts such as the one I am reading now from a laptop, psychoanalysis is by necessity, against the tide.

And it always was, even when it seemed to be a fad. Only when we go against the tide can we hear some things like the crackling noise of the needle on an old vinyl record, a remnant as anachronic and mysterious as the words with which psychoanalysis is accustomed to work.

A Night in the Museum

I like to think of each conference as being *located* in a place. And this place[15] has a lot of meaning for me.

I was here thirty years ago, when I didn't know I was going to become a psychoanalyst. I came with a close friend of mine who died just after our trip. His death had a lot to do with my decision to become a psychoanalyst and the fact that I am here today.

I am here also because of Felix de Mendelsohn. Both have been guides in a way: *Into the lightness*.

This place is usually empty. The furniture and objects of Freud and his family are in London, in the other Freud Museum. Stripped of objects, this place is what it is.

The idea of place as emptiness is central for a project like *Geographies*. Unlike Hell, space is made for what is missing here, which is precisely what remains hidden in virtual spaces.

This museum is more real than the one in London, where Freud lived for only a few months. It was here that Freud heard stories allowing him to develop psychoanalysis.

The truth shown here is that of the *Catastrophe*, the disaster brought about by Nazism. In this sense it is a *lieu de memoire*.[16] The emptiness that remains is a testament to that Hell, that open wound.

---

15   Vienna's Freud Museum.
16   Pierre Nora, *Les Lieux de mémoire*, cit., in Joanne Morra, cf. n. 17.

Memory and emptiness also belong to Felix, who dreamed of this gathering, and whose absence marks everything that we have been able to say.

The caretakers of the museum have wisely included an interlocution among contemporary artists,[17] experts of emptiness. So, I would like to finish by showing some works of a contemporary Latin American artist. In this place, so European, images of where psychoanalysis has settled with unusual force will be seen for a fleeting moment — as in *Snapchat*.

The photographs belong to Luis González Palma, one of the most important Latin American photographers. His work, as anachronic as that of Borges or Freud, is a sort of *Treaty on the Gaze*, and the effect of a fertile dialogue with psychoanalysis can be felt.

At this point, the analyst opens his eyes and without ceasing to listen, gazes.

---

17   Joanne Morra, 'Seemengly empty. Freud at Berggasse 19, a conceptual museum in Vienna', Journal of Visual Culture, 12, 1 (2013).

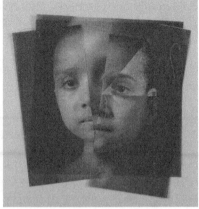

Luis González Palma, from the series
Möbius, 2013-2014.

Luis González Palma, from the series
Möbius, 2013-2014.

Luis González Palma, from the series
Möbius, 2013-2014.

Luis González Palma, from the series
Möbius, 2013-2014.

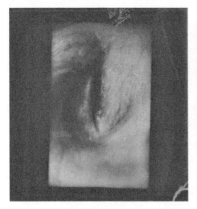

Luis González Palma, from the series
"Nupcias de soledad"
(Nuptials of solitude)

Luis González Palma, from the series
"Nupcias de soledad"
(Nuptials of solitude)

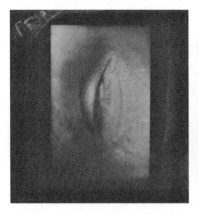

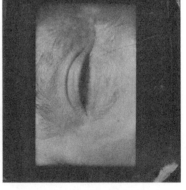

Luis González Palma, from the series
"Nupcias de soledad"
(Nuptials of solitude)

Luis González Palma, from the series
"Nupcias de soledad"
(Nuptials of solitude)

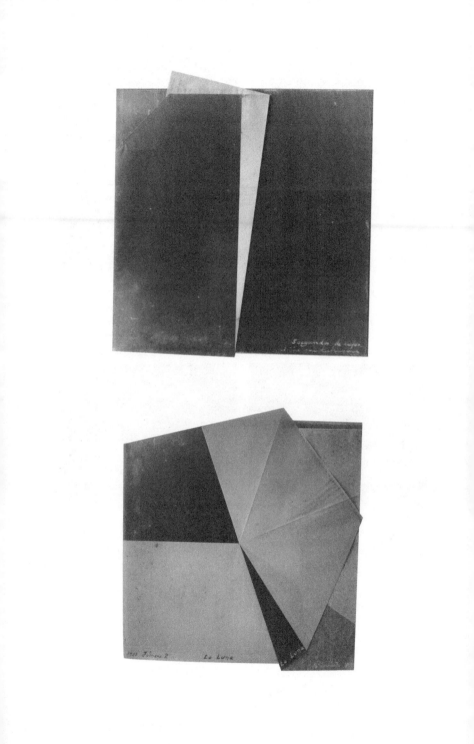

Pages 90-91: Luis González Palma, from the series Koan, 2016.

"THE TIME IS OUT OF JOINT". NEW SUBJECTIVITIES

Lorena Preta

I begin with this very famous line from William Shakespeare's Hamlet because the significance and implication that it contains, help describe the impression of de-centering, of deconstruction, which we live and experience in today's times.

This phenomenon is caused by various factors and while it is happening worldwide, and partly as a result of globalization itself, it is perceived in different ways, in the various cultures and countries of the world.

It may be represented, especially in relationship to the new means of communication and social organization that characterize our times, to such a large extent, that we may possibly consider finding ourselves at the dawn of a "new subject".

A dislocated subject, indeed, which has lost its customary centre and which finds itself living in an unstable way, the experience of self, of its body, of its history, of the community's history to which it belongs, as if it were involved in a spatial and time move, alienating it from the internal place appointed to ensure a sense of belonging.

However, this phenomenon is not only marked by elements of crisis, for it makes it, at the same time, a bearer of deep albeit difficult transformations, to be measured in their extent and consequences.

We can think of this as a hybrid, the fruit of diverse cultures blending. It is useless to think in terms of a clash of civilizations, Islamic versus Western or vice versa. In reality, Western culture won some time ago but has defused itself in a viral manner, creating *new formations*, which are apparently integrated but really fight each other for survival, just like desperate antibodies of a system that absorbed them long ago.

Perhaps it will not always be like this but as has already occurred in past centuries, new multiform and complex cultures will spring forth.

Going back to our famous quotation by Shakespeare, we may also find that it contains an appeal for "justice" that Hamlet takes upon himself in the drama, and which has also strong implications for our topic of discussion. In fact, the Prince believes that it is up to him to put things back into their proper place, to realign time on its axes, through revenge.

I shall try to explain in what way this is related to our times and to the "dislocated subject", which I will attempt to describe. I will take as a 'figure' representing this phenomenon, the event which is currently affecting us the most: terrorism. Even if it is now difficult to talk of events associated with radical Islam, or Islamic extremism in a politically correct way, I hope nonetheless, that these definitions, which are so rapidly being worn out by overuse, may be of support to our discussion.

In the terrible events that we are witnessing, we see the appearance of an individual who is prepared to sacrifice his/her life and the many lives of those considered enemies and infidels. This individual will use technology to communicate and disseminate the belief of his/her religion, which has been re-interpreted in a twisted manner. Yet what is mostly striking above all, at least for me, is that as a result of the suicide attacks, these individuals will utilize their bodies, fully aware that besides death, they will undergo horrible mutilation. To what representation of self does all this correspond?

Fethi Benslama, psychoanalyst of Tunisian origins, uses the term "surmusulman", to describe this type of subject. A person who does not feel that he is "enough of a Muslim", and who obstinately seeks to be a super-Muslim, as if his identity required affirmation through the struggle for a "justice of identity", that would heal what he feels to be a "wound of Islamic idealism".

It would appear that nothing is sufficient to affirm and live one's affiliation to Islam. We witness the emergence of a real and true "obsession", that translates into forced rituals and into what is defined as the radicalization of communal and religious behaviors. An internal enemy is created even before an external one, which in psychoanalytical terms, we refer to as an archaic and persecutory superego.

As Westerners, believed to be the enemy, we not only experience the fragility of a constant, global and generalized threat but we are also reduced to a generic "category", which may be generally attacked without specific reason. In turn, we also apply the same diminishing identification with a suspected enemy, of any Muslim or Arab, without taking into consideration any distinction, and confusing geographical areas, historical events and political situations. My same argument, at this moment, simplifies in a generalizing manner, a complex and articulate issue that would deserve an in-depth exposition which is not possible here.

Let us clarify some preliminary points. We know that the appalling colonial policies, created fertile ground for this hate. These situations, though related to the past, are psychologically inherited by the new generations to which today's terrorists belong (and whom we know are for the most part, young persons aged between 14 and 25), based on a psychic phenomenon termed in psychoanalysis, as *transgenerational transmission*, and that can sometimes skip even two or three generations.

An individual may therefore find himself, indirectly and more or less consciously experiencing events that belong not to him, but rather to his parents, grandparents or even more distant relatives. This may not be ascribed to the deliberate transmission on the part of family members of past events, but rather to the unconscious communication of painful and traumatic experiences. We often see in fact, that these persons are second generation Muslims, and that their families are more or less "integrated" in the country hosting them, sometimes at the price of erasing their past lives and related suffering, prior to their immigration.

Furthermore, we cannot close our eyes to the fact that violence perpetuated by the Western world, is now carried out in the name of war with merciless bombardments, despite the famous technology which should avoid the killing of civilians, but which instead brings about the massacre of helpless and inert populations, women, children and hospitalized patients.

Much can be said also on the potential future perspectives that are offered to these people in the countries hosting them. Generally, we know that this is also applicable to those Westerners who really have nothing to do with the culture of terrorists but who experience a sense of alienation leading them to identify with their anger. This is certainly due to their specific life stories but also to the fact that they find it impossible to have satisfying potential future perspectives; more in general, it is also due to the lack of ideals that is so often discussed.

On this basis, hate and the pursuit of revenge, as we said at the beginning with reference to Shakespeare's words, are the drive behind the attempt to realign time on its axes, to seek justice. This justice however, is not a human one but rather it has only one judge and point of reference, an unforgiving God who punishes enemies and rewards the faithful.

Therefore, in order to attain these rewards and to reach this God, it is necessary to believe in an afterlife that will erase their past. This afterlife will not necessarily reward a lifetime of righteousness and conformation to religious norms but rather it will come as *an enlightenment*, a sort of launch into another dimension, the dimension of Heaven, where none of the world's history has any further meaning.

An image tragically comparable to the explosion of the body of the suicide bomber that disappears, mutilated and dismembered, unrecognizable because the human identity until that point was not the real identity, neither physical nor psychic. Indeed only the identity conquered through sacrifice has value and is a guarantee of his belonging to God.

So what is the time in which these young people are living? The present is not, as it should be, a consequence of the past, in an articulate and complex manner but rather the connection to past events is a sort of hallucination; it is traumatic as if the past were still there in the present time, without having gone through any transformation and determining the present, beyond what is necessary.

The future on the other hand is sucked back in this way, emptied of its guarantees for change in the sense of evolution, which should characterize it but rather it is pressed onto the present or thrown into an artificial imaginary, which holds nothing of what is known or thinkable to this point. An apocalyptic future which can take place only in the post-catastrophe.

Terrorism provides an extreme example of course but it surely contains even too many expressions of the contemporary uneasiness and numerous connections to that dislocation which we are seeking to describe.

More in general we may say that the behaviors we observe in current society, even within different countries in the world, appear to be characterized by a tendency to "act the unconscious", as if this were reversed on the outside and as if the necessary distinction between interior world and external reality were lost, and the multiple elements, characterizing the subject were emptied and fragmented, in much the way that psychoanalytic thinking ascribes to psychotic thinking.

The constitution of the psyche based on the interaction between the psychic singularity and the social system, should necessarily go through an appropriation of the common meanings contained in the storage of the *social imaginary*, which in turn produces them, in a relationship of mutual transformation. However, in order to enact this process, it is necessary to have a place which can work as a space of elaboration, escaping the compulsion to act; a place where the subject may stay and recognize himself, while now subjectivity appears to always be dislocated elsewhere, in an extended physical space, which at this point contains both the inside and the outside without continuity. A whole which is present, horizontal and simultaneous.

In this dynamics, how does the representation of the body change?

Indeed, where does the body go? It often seems that we are witnessing the creation of a factual counter-reality, which takes a distance from the bodily experience as we know it and carries us in another dimension, similar to an hallucination, where meeting with reality is avoided because it is too painful.

As can also be seen in a lot of contemporary art or in some adolescent body rituals, an altered body is carried on the scene, distorted, made unrecognizable, with its parts and organs used in unusual manners. The bodies which we come upon in our psychoanalytical offices, in mass media, on the web, do not appear to be searching for an authentic bodily self, belonging to an identifiable individual but rather they seem to correspond to a collective imaginary, which magnifies them and removes their subjective features.

We witness phenomena of embodied dislocations where any sense is completely flattened on the body absorbing it, as in a black hole, from which it is difficult to extract meanings and where any processing seems impossible, while at the same time, some disembodied dislocations propel the body lights years away, in a virtual reality which projects it as a hologram, unreachable on the scene.

However, these phenomena should not be pathologized, although it is necessary not to accept them without criticism but rather they should be disarticulated and placed in relation to their deep meaning and mostly, they should be adequately described, trying to create a time "into the joint", if ever history lived one.

AUTHORS

PAOLO FABBRI is director of the International Center for Semiotic Sciences (CiSS), Urbino University. He teaches Semiotics of Art for the Master of Visual Art, Libera Università Internazionale degli Studi Sociali (LUISS), Rome. Director of the International Semiotic Laboratory at Venice (LISAV); director of the collection "Segnature", Mimesis, Milan. Visiting professor at the University of California, S. Diego (UCSD); visiting researcher at the University of Toronto. Directeur d'Etudes associé at the École des hautes études en sciences sociales (EHESS); professeur invité at the Université Sorbonne, Paris V and Paris VII; Directeur de Programme at the Collège International de Philosophie, Paris. Former President of the Institut de la Pensée Contemporaine, Université Sorbonne, Paris VII. His books and articles have been published and translated in many languages. Among his latest publications: *Tactica de los signos* (Barcellona: Gedisa Editora, 1999); *Elogio di Babele* (Rome: Meltemi, 2003); *Segni del tempo* (Rome: Meltemi, 2004); *La Svolta Semiotica* (Rome: Laterza, 2005; with G. Marrone), *Semiotica in nuce: un'antologia*, 2 voll. (Rome: Meltemi, 2000/1); *Fellinerie* (Rimini: Guaraldi ed., 2016).

GOHAR HOMAYOUNPOUR is an author and a psychoanalyst who belongs to the International Psychoanalytic Association, American Psychoanalytic Association, and the National Association for the Advancement of Psychoanalysis. She is founder and director of the Freudian Group of Tehran, where she is training and supervising psychoanalysts. Lecturer at Shahid Beheshti University. Dr. Homayounpour is a member of the scientific board at the Freud Museum in Vienna, and of the IPA Group Geographies of Psychoanalysis. Homayounpour has published various psychoanalytic articles, including in the International and Canadian journal of psychoanalysis. Her book "Doing Psychoanalysis in Tehran", the MIT Press August 2012, won the Gradiva award and it has been translated into various languages.

Mariano Horenstein is training analyst (IPA). Past Chief editor of "Calibán", official Journal of the Latin American Psychoanalytical Federation. He has lectured in many Latin American countries, in the EU and Iran. He has recently published the book *Psychoanalysis in minor language*. Some of his articles have been translated into six languages. He has received international awards, such as M. Bergwerk, Freud (Psychoanalysis and Culture), Elise Hayman Award for the study of Holocaust and Genocide (IPA) and A. Garma (Spanish Association of Neuropsychiatry).

Vittorio Lingiardi, M.D., is a psychiatrist and psychoanalyst. He is Full Professor of Dynamic Psychology and past Director (2006-2013) of the Clinical Psychology Specialization Program, Faculty of Medicine and Psychology, Sapienza University of Rome (Italy). His research interests include diagnostic assessment of personality disorders, process-outcome research in psychoanalysis and psychotherapy, gender identity and sexual orientation. He has published widely on these topics, including articles in the "American Journal of Psychiatry", "World Psychiatry", "Contemporary Psychoanalysis", "International Journal of Psychoanalysis", "Psychoanalytic Dialogues", and "Psychoanalytic Psychology". He is currently coordinating with Nancy McWilliams the new edition of the *Psychodynamic Diagnostic Manual* (PDM-2, Guilford Press, June 2017). He is Chief Editor of the series "Psychiatry, Neuroscience, Psychotherapy" for Raffaello Cortina (Milan, Italy). He is collaborator of the cultural insert "Domenica Sole 24 ore" and of the magazine "Venerdì di Repubblica", where he writes the weekly feature "Psycho" on cinema and psychoanalysis.

Lorena Preta is the Director of the International Research Group "Geographies of Psychoanalysis". Full member of the Italian Psychoanalytical Society (SPI) and of the International Psychoanalytical Association (IPA). Past editor in chief of the journal "Psyche" (Journal of psychoanalysis and culture of the Italian Psychoanalytical Society). Scientific consultant and director for many years of *Spoletoscienza* (Meetings of science and culture at the Festival of Two Worlds in Spoleto). She conceived and edited the series "Italian Lessons" for Laterza. Author of many publications including: *La narrazione delle origini* (1991); *Immagini e metafore della scienza* (1993); *Nuove geometrie della mente* (1999). She has recently published the books: *Geographies of Psychoanalysis. Encounters between Cultures in Tehran* (Mimesis International, 2015), *La brutalità delle cose*. *Trasformazioni psichiche della realtà* (Mimesis, 2015) and *Cartographies of the Unconscious. A new Atlas for Psychoanalysis* (Mimesis International, 2016).

MARCELO VIÑAR is a doctor and psychoanalyst. He has published many articles related to identity and adolescence, and volumes like *Fracturas de Memoria* (1993); *Psicoanalizar hoy* (2002); *Mundos Adolescentes y Vértigo Civilizatorio* (2009). He is Full Member of the Asociación Psicoanalítica del Uruguay and Member of the International Psychoanalytic Association. He has been Associate Professor in the Department of Medical Education of the Faculty of Medicine, Universidad de la República Uruguay (Udelar); now he coordinates research groups on adolescence, marginality and juvenile deliquency. He is also Advisor of the Consejo Nacional de Educación on issues of healthy coexistence and prevention of violence.

JEANNE WOLFF BERNSTEIN teaches at the Sigmund Freud University in Vienna, at PINC and at The New York University Postdoctoral Program of Psychoanalysis and Psychotherapy in New York. She was president and training analyst at the Psychoanalytic Institute of Northern California (PINC) in San Francisco. She was Fulbright Freud Visiting Scholar in Psychoanalysis and chair of the Scientific Advisory Board at the Freud Museum, Vienna. She is member of the Wiener Arbeitskreis für Psychoanalyse. She has published numerous articles on the comparison between psychoanalysis, visual arts and cinema. Her most recent publications include: 'Psychoanalytic Tattoos/Hysteria', in *Body Image and Identity in Contemporary Societies* (Routledge, 2015) and the chapter 'Between the Artist's Studio and the Psychoanalytic Office: A Comparison of Lucian Freud's and Sigmund Freud's Interior Space', in *Private Utopia, Cultural Setting of the Interior in the 19th and 20 th century* (De Gruyter, 2015). Her latest essay, titled 'Living between two languages, a bi-focal perspective', has been published in *Locating Ourselves: Immigration in the Analytic Encounter* (Routledge, 2016).

MIMESIS GROUP

www.mimesis-group.com

MIMESIS INTERNATIONAL

www.mimesisinternational.com

info@mimesisinternational.com

MIMESIS EDIZIONI

www.mimesisedizioni.it

mimesis@mimesisedizioni.it

ÉDITIONS MIMÉSIS

www.editionsmimesis.fr

info@editionsmimesis.fr

MIMESIS COMMUNICATION

www.mim-c.net

MIMESIS EU

www.mim-eu.com

Printed by Booksfactory – Szczecin (Poland) in February 2018